SIMPLIFIED DIFFERENTIAL CALCULUS

Derivatives and Limits with Many Worked Examples

Kingsley Augustine

Printed by Amazon KDP

Table of Contents

PREFACE

Simplified Differential Calculus is a book that contains topics under differential calculus. This book serves as a useful companion to students in high schools, colleges and universities. It is a valuable textbook for students who want to write entrance test or examination into colleges and universities. This book consists of step-by-step explanation of topics presented in a way that is easy for students to understand. It contains very many worked examples and many self-assessment exercises to ensure that students get a mastery of each topic covered. The answers to the exercises are provided at the end of the book.

What makes this book a unique mathematical asset, is its detailed step by step approach in explaining the topics covered in this branch of mathematics. Instead of solving questions by going straight to the point, leaving you confused and frustrated, this textbook teaches you in simple English, explaining each step taken at a time. Thus, allowing anyone, regardless of their experience in calculus, to understand each topic with ease, and hence make mathematics more interesting.

I give all thanks and Glory to God Almighty, for giving me the grace to write this book. I also wish to express my deep appreciation to my wife Mrs. Mercy Augustine for her patience, understanding and encouragement when I was writing this book. I also thank my children, Dora, Merit and Elvis for their moral support.

Kingsley Augustine.

CHAPTER 1
LIMIT OF A FUNCTION

The concept of limits is very important in differential calculus. A function has a limiting value when its variable approaches a certain value. For example, if the limiting value of f(x) as x approaches 4 is 16, it is written as:

$$\lim_{x \to 4} f(x) = 16$$

In evaluating limit, some problems are simply solved by just putting in the values of the variables, while some problems are solved by applying certain rules.

Some important limits

1. $\lim_{x \to 0} \dfrac{\sin x}{x} = 1$ and $\lim_{x \to 0} \dfrac{\tan x}{x} = 1$ (Or $\lim_{x \to 0} \dfrac{\sin ax}{ax} = 1$ and $\lim_{x \to 0} \dfrac{\tan ax}{ax} = 1$)

2. $\lim_{x \to 0} \dfrac{1 - \cos x}{x} = 0$ and $\lim_{x \to 0} \dfrac{1 - \cos a x}{x} = 0$

3. $\lim_{x \to \infty} \left(1 + \dfrac{1}{x}\right)^x = e$

4. $\lim_{x \to 0} \dfrac{a^x - 1}{a^x} = 1$

5. $\lim_{x \to 0} \dfrac{e^x - 1}{x} = 1$

6. $\lim_{x \to 0} \dfrac{1 + x}{x} = 1$

7. $\lim_{x \to a} \dfrac{x^n - a^n}{x - a} = na^{n-1}$

8. $\lim_{x \to 0} \dfrac{a^x - 1}{x} = \ln a$

9. $\lim_{x \to \infty} \dfrac{\ln x}{x} = 0$

10. $\lim_{x \to \infty} x^{\frac{1}{x}} = 0$

11. $\lim_{x \to 0} (1 + x)^{\frac{1}{x}} = e$

12. $\lim_{x \to 0} (1 + \sin x)^{\frac{1}{x}} = e$

13. $\lim_{x \to a} c = c$

Examples

1. Evaluate $\lim\limits_{x \to 0} 3x^3 - 5x^2 + 2x + 6$

<u>Solution</u>

$\lim\limits_{x \to 0} 3x^3 - 5x^2 + 2x + 6$

Simply substitute zero for x in the given expression. This gives:

$= 3(0^3) - 5(0^2) + 2(0) + 6$

$= 0 - 0 + 0 + 6$

$= 6$

2. Evaluate $\lim\limits_{x \to 0} \dfrac{x^2 + 3x - 11}{4x^2 - 5x - 5}$

<u>Solution</u>

$\lim\limits_{x \to 0} \dfrac{x^2 + 3x - 11}{4x^2 - 5x - 5}$

Substituting 0 for x into the expression gives:

$= \dfrac{0^2 + 3(0) - 11}{4(0)^2 - 5(0) - 5}$

$= \dfrac{0 + 0 - 11}{0 - 0 - 5}$

$= \dfrac{-11}{-5}$

$= \dfrac{11}{5}$

$= 2\dfrac{1}{5}$

3. Evaluate $\lim\limits_{x \to 4} \dfrac{x^2 - 2x - 8}{x - 4}$

<u>Solution</u>

A close look at the expression shows that if 4 is substituted for x, it will give $\dfrac{0}{0}$. This has no value as it is indeterminate. Therefore, in order to solve a limit such as this, we have to factorize the denominator and then simplify the expression. This is done as follows:

$\lim\limits_{x \to 4} \dfrac{x^2 - 2x - 8}{x - 4} = \lim\limits_{x \to 4} \dfrac{(x+2)(x-4)}{x - 4}$

Cancelling out $(x - 4)$ gives:

$\lim\limits_{x \to 4} (x + 2)$

We now substitute 4 for x to obtain our final answer as follows:

$\lim\limits_{x \to 4} (x + 2) = 4 + 2$

$= 6$

Therefore, $\lim\limits_{x \to 4} \dfrac{x^2 + x - 8}{x - 4} = 6$

4. Evaluate $\displaystyle\lim_{x\to2} \frac{x^2-4}{x-2}$

Solution

This is similar to example 3 above since substituting 2 for x in the expression will $\frac{0}{0}$ which has no

value. Hence we factorize the numerator and simplify as follows:

$\displaystyle\lim_{x\to2} \frac{x^2-4}{x-2} = \lim_{x\to2} \frac{(x-2)(x+2)}{x-2}$ [Note that $x^2 - 4 = x^2 - 2^2$ and recall that $a^2 - b^2 = (a + b)(a - b)$]

Cancelling out $(x-2)$ gives:

$\displaystyle\lim_{x\to2} (x+2)$

We now substitute 2 for x to obtain our final answer as follows:

$\displaystyle\lim_{x\to2} (x+2) = 2 + 2$

$= 4$

Therefore, $\displaystyle\lim_{x\to2} \frac{x^2-4}{x-2} = 4$

5. Evaluate $\displaystyle\lim_{x\to0} (2x-5)(x+2)(3x-1)$

Solution

$\displaystyle\lim_{x\to0} (2x-5)(x+2)(3x-1)$

Substituting 0 for x in the expression gives:

$\displaystyle\lim_{x\to0} (2x-5)(x+2)(3x-1) = [2(0)-5][(0)+2][3(0)-1]$

$= (-5)(2)(-1)$

$= 10$

6. Evaluate $\displaystyle\lim_{x\to\infty} \frac{x^3+2x^2+5x+3}{x^3+x^2+3x+7}$

Solution

In this case of x approaching infinity, we evaluate it by first dividing each term in the numerator
and denominator by the variable having the highest exponent (power). Hence we divide each
term by x^3. This is done as follows:

$\displaystyle\lim_{x\to\infty} \frac{x^3+2x^2+5x+3}{x^3+x^2+3x+7} = \lim_{x\to\infty} \frac{\frac{x^3}{x^3}+\frac{2x^2}{x^3}+\frac{5x}{x^3}+\frac{3}{x^3}}{\frac{x^3}{x^3}+\frac{x^2}{x^3}+\frac{3x}{x^3}+\frac{7}{x^3}}$

$= \displaystyle\lim_{x\to\infty} \frac{1+\frac{2}{x}+\frac{5}{x^2}+\frac{3}{x^3}}{1+\frac{1}{x}+\frac{3}{x^2}+\frac{7}{x^3}}$

$$= \frac{1 + \frac{2}{\infty} + \frac{5}{\infty^2} + \frac{3}{\infty^3}}{1 + \frac{1}{\infty} + \frac{3}{\infty^2} + \frac{7}{\infty^3}}$$

$$= \frac{1 + 0 + 0 + 0}{1 + 0 + 0 + 0}$$ (Note that a number divided by ∞ gives 0)

$$= \frac{1}{1}$$

$$= 1$$

7. Evaluate $\lim\limits_{x \to \infty} \dfrac{2x^4 - 3x^2 + 8x - 1}{x^4 - 5x + 3}$

Solution

The variable in its highest exponent (power) is x^4. Hence we divide each term by x^4 as follows:

$$\lim\limits_{x \to \infty} \frac{2x^4 - 3x^2 + 8x - 1}{x^4 - 5x + 3} = \lim\limits_{x \to \infty} \frac{\frac{2x^4}{x^4} - \frac{3x^2}{x^4} + \frac{8x}{x^4} - \frac{1}{x^4}}{\frac{x^4}{x^4} - \frac{5x}{x^4} + \frac{3}{x^4}}$$

$$= \lim\limits_{x \to \infty} \frac{2 - \frac{3}{x^2} + \frac{8}{x^3} - \frac{1}{x^4}}{1 - \frac{5}{x^3} + \frac{3}{x^4}}$$

$$= \frac{2 - \frac{3}{\infty} + \frac{8}{\infty} - \frac{1}{\infty}}{1 - \frac{5}{\infty} + \frac{3}{\infty}}$$

$$= \frac{2 - 0 + 0 - 0}{1 - 0 + 0}$$ (Note that a number divided by ∞ gives 0)

$$= \frac{2}{1}$$

$$= 2$$

8. Evaluate $\lim\limits_{x \to 4} \dfrac{2x^2 - 7x - 4}{x^2 - 3x - 4}$

Solution

If 4 is substituted for x in the function above, it will give $\dfrac{0}{0}$ which is an indeterminate value.

Hence we factorize the expression and simplify as follows:

$$\lim\limits_{x \to 4} \frac{2x^2 - 7x - 4}{x^2 - 3x - 4} = \lim\limits_{x \to 4} \frac{(2x + 1)(x - 4)}{(x + 1)(x - 4)}$$

Cancelling out $(x - 4)$ gives:

$$\lim\limits_{x \to 4} \frac{2x + 1}{x + 1}$$

If 9 is substituted for x in the expression above, it will give $\frac{0}{0}$ which is not the desired answer. Hence a way to go around this problem is to multiply the top and bottom by the conjugate of the surd at the top. The conjugate of $3 - \sqrt{x}$ is $3 + \sqrt{x}$ (only a difference in their middle signs). Hence we multiply top and bottom by $3 + \sqrt{x}$ and simplify as follows:

$$\lim_{x \to 9} \frac{3 - \sqrt{x}}{9 - x} = \lim_{x \to 9} \frac{(3 - \sqrt{x})(3 + \sqrt{x})}{(9 - x)(3 + \sqrt{x})}$$

$$= \lim_{x \to 9} \frac{3^2 - (\sqrt{x})^2}{(9 - x)(3 + \sqrt{x})} \quad \text{(Note that the top was simplified by using } (a - b)(a + b) = a^2 - b^2)$$

$$= \lim_{x \to 9} \frac{9 - x}{(9 - x)(3 + \sqrt{x})}$$

$$= \lim_{x \to 9} \frac{1}{(3 + \sqrt{x})} \quad \text{(Since } 9 - x \text{ cancels out)}$$

We now substitute 9 for x as follows:

$$\lim_{x \to 9} \frac{1}{(3 + \sqrt{x})} = \frac{1}{(3 + \sqrt{9})}$$

$$= \frac{1}{3 + 3}$$

$$= \frac{1}{6}$$

14. Evaluate $\lim_{x \to 1} \dfrac{x^2 - 1}{x^5 - 1}$

Solution

If 2 is substituted for x in the expression above, it will give $\frac{0}{0}$ which is not a good answer. Hence a way to go around this problem is to divide the top and bottom by $x - 1$ (i.e. the difference between the variable and 1). This is done as follows:

$$\lim_{x \to 1} \frac{x^2 - 1}{x^5 - 1} = \lim_{x \to 1} \frac{\dfrac{x^2 - 1}{x - 1}}{\dfrac{x^5 - 1}{x - 1}} \quad \text{(Note that this has not changed the original fraction)}$$

Note that $\lim_{x \to a} \dfrac{x^n - a^n}{x - a} = na^{n-1}$. With this rule we now simplify the expression above as follows:

$$\lim_{x \to 1} \frac{\dfrac{x^2 - 1}{x - 1}}{\dfrac{x^5 - 1}{x - 1}} = \frac{2 \times 1^{(2 - 1)}}{5 \times 1^{(5 - 1)}}$$

$$= \frac{2 \times 1^1}{5 \times 1^5}$$

$$= \frac{2}{5}$$

Continuity of a function

A function is said to be continuous if the three conditions below are satisfied.

1. f(a) exists

2. $\lim_{x \to a}$ f(x) exists

3. $\lim_{x \to a}$ f(x) = f(a)   (i.e. if the values of conditions 1 and 2 above are equal)

Examples

1. Determine if the function f(x) = $2x^2 - 8x + 5$ is continuous at the point $x = -1$

Solution

When $x = -1$, the f(−1) is obtained as follows:

$$f(x) = 2x^2 - 8x + 5$$
$$f(-1) = 2(-1)^2 - 8(-1) + 5$$
$$= 2 + 8 + 5$$
$$= 15$$

Since f(−1) = 15, it means that f(−1) exists.

The next step is to find the value of $\lim_{x \to -1}$ f(x) as follows:

$$\lim_{x \to -1} 2x^2 - 8x + 5 = 2(-1)^2 - 8(-1) + 5$$
$$= 2 + 8 + 5$$
$$= 15$$

Hence f(−1) = $\lim_{x \to -1}$ f(x) = 15

Therefore, the function is continuous.

2. Determine if the function f(x) = $\dfrac{2x + 1}{x^2 - 3x + 7}$ is continuous at $x = 2$

Solution

When $x = 2$, the f(2) is obtained as follows:

$$f(x) = \frac{2x + 1}{x^2 - 3x + 7}$$
$$f(2) = \frac{2(2) + 1}{2^2 - 3(2) + 7}$$
$$= \frac{4 + 1}{4 - 6 + 7}$$
$$= \frac{5}{5}$$
$$= 1$$

Since f(2) = 1, it means that f(2) exists.

The next step is to find the value of $\lim_{x \to 2}$ f(x) as follows:

$$\lim_{x \to 2} \frac{2x + 1}{x^2 - 3x + 7} = \frac{2(2) + 1}{2^2 - 3(2) + 7}$$

$$= \frac{4+1}{4-6+7}$$

$$= \frac{5}{5}$$

$$= 1$$

Hence $f(2) = \underset{x \to 2}{lim} f(x) = 1$

Therefore, the function is continuous.

3. Determine if the function $f(x) = \dfrac{2x^2 - 8}{x+4}$ is continuous at $x = -4$.

When $x = -4$, the f(−4) is obtained as follows:

$$f(x) = \frac{2x^2 - 8}{x+4}$$

$$f(-4) = \frac{2(-4^2) - 8}{-4+4}$$

$$= \frac{2(16) - 8}{0}$$

$$= \frac{24}{0} \quad \text{(Undefined)}$$

Hence f(−4) is undefined, and does not exist. This shows that the function is not continuous. It is discontinuous as $x = -4$.

4. Determine if the function $f(x) = \dfrac{x^2 - 9}{x - 3}$ is continuous at $x = 3$.

When $x = 3$, the f(3) is obtained as follows:

$$f(x) = \frac{x^2 - 9}{x-3}$$

$$f(3) = \frac{3^2 - 9}{3-3}$$

$$= \frac{0}{0} \quad \text{(This has no value)}$$

Hence f(3) does not exist.

Let us determine the value of $\underset{x \to 3}{lim} f(x)$ as follows:

$$\underset{x \to 3}{lim} \frac{x^2 - 9}{x-3} = \underset{x \to 3}{lim} \frac{(x-3)(x+3)}{x-3}$$

$$= \underset{x \to 3}{lim} (x+3) \quad \text{(Since } x-3 \text{ cancels out)}$$

$$= 3+3 \quad \text{(When 3 is substituted for } x\text{)}$$

$$= 6$$

Hence, f(3) has no value while $\underset{x \to 3}{lim} f(x) = 6$

This shows that $f(3) \neq \underset{x \to 3}{lim} f(x)$

Therefore the function discontinuous.

5. Test for the continuity of the function: $f(x) = \begin{cases} -5x + 7 & \text{if } x > 1 \\ x^2 + 2 & \text{if } x \leq 1 \end{cases}$

Solution

$$f(x) = \begin{cases} -5x + 7 & \text{if } x > 1 \\ x^2 + 2 & \text{if } x \leq 1 \end{cases}$$

When $x = 1$, we use the expression $x^2 + 2$ to evaluate f(1). Note that $x \leq 1$ means $x < 1$ or $x = 1$.

Hence, $f(x) = x^2 + 2$ (for $x = 1$)

$\qquad f(1) = 1^2 + 2$

$\qquad\qquad = 3$

Since f(1) = 3, it means that f(1) exist.

Let us now determine the limiting value of f(x).

If x approaches 1 from the left, which is $x \leq 1$ (left hand elbow) we write it as $\lim\limits_{x \to 1-} f(x)$, and we pick the expression given by:

$\qquad f(x) = x^2 + 2$

Hence, $\lim\limits_{x \to 1} f(x) = 1^2 + 3$

$\qquad\qquad = 3$

If x approaches 1 from the right, which is $x > 1$ (right hand elbow), we write it as $\lim\limits_{x \to 1+} f(x)$, and we pick the expression given by:

$\qquad f(x) = -5x + 7$

Hence, $\lim\limits_{x \to 1} f(x) = -5(1) + 7$

$\qquad\qquad = 2$

Hence, $\lim\limits_{x \to 1-} f(x) = 3$ while $\lim\limits_{x \to 1+} f(x) = 2$. They are not equal. This shows that $\lim\limits_{x \to 1} f(x)$ does not exist. Therefore, the function is not continuous.

6. Determine the continuity of the function: $f(x) = \begin{cases} x^2 & \text{if } x \geq -2 \\ x+6 & \text{if } x < -2 \end{cases}$

Solution

$$f(x) = \begin{cases} x^2 & \text{if } x \geq -2 \\ x+6 & \text{if } x < -2 \end{cases}$$

A direct way of determining the continuity of functions such as these is to find the limits of the two expressions in the function as x tends to the values given in the question.

Therefore, when x tends to -2 in the function $f(x) = x^2$, we have:

$\qquad f(x) = x^2$

Hence, $\lim\limits_{x \to -2} f(x) = (-2)^2$

$\qquad\qquad = 4$

Also, when x tends to -2 in the function $f(x) = x + 6$, we have:

$\qquad f(x) = x + 6$

Hence, $\lim\limits_{x \to -2} f(x) = -2 + 6$

$\qquad\qquad = 4$

Hence, $\lim\limits_{x \to -2} x^2 = \lim\limits_{x \to -2} x + 6 = 4$. Their limits give the same value. This shows that $\lim\limits_{x \to -2} f(x)$ exist. Therefore, the function is continuous.

7. Determine if the function below is continuous or not.

$$f(x) = \begin{cases} \dfrac{x^2 - 16}{x + 4} & \text{if } x \geq -4 \\ \dfrac{x + 4}{2x - 3} & \text{if } x < -4 \end{cases}$$

Solution

As x tends to -4 in the function $f(x) = \dfrac{x^2 - 16}{x + 4}$ we simplify as follows:

$$f(x) = \frac{(x + 4)(x - 4)}{x + 4}$$

Hence, $\lim\limits_{x \to -4} f(x) = (x - 4)$ (Note that $(x + 4)$ cancels out)

$$= -4 - 4$$
$$= -8$$

Also, when x tends to -4 in the function $f(x) = \dfrac{x + 4}{2x - 3}$, we have:

$$\lim\limits_{x \to -4} f(x) = \frac{-4 + 4}{2(-4) - 3}$$
$$= \frac{-4 + 4}{-8 - 3}$$
$$= \frac{0}{-11}$$
$$= 0$$

Their limits give different values. This shows that $\lim\limits_{x \to -4} f(x)$ does not exist. Therefore, the function is not continuous.

8. If $f(x) = \begin{cases} \dfrac{x^2 - 4}{x - 2} \\ 4 \text{ if } x = 2 \end{cases}$ test for the continuity of the function at $x = 2$.

Solution

$$f(x) = \begin{cases} \dfrac{x^2 - 4}{x - 2} \\ 4 \text{ if } x = 2 \end{cases}$$

Let us find the limits of the two expressions in the function as x tends 2.
From the first expression, as x tends to 2 we have:

$$f(x) = \frac{x^2 - 4}{x - 2}$$

Hence, $\lim\limits_{x \to 2} f(x) = \dfrac{(x - 2)(x + 2)}{x - 2}$ (When the numerator is factorized)

$\lim\limits_{x \to 2} f(x) = (x + 2)$ ($x - 2$ has cancelled out)

$\lim\limits_{x \to 2} f(x) = 2 + 2$

15

= 4

Also, when x tends to 2 in the function f(x) = 4, we have:

f(x) = 4

Hence, $\lim\limits_{x \to 2} 4 = 4$ (Since $\lim\limits_{x \to a} c = c$)

The question also tells us that when x = 2, f(x) = 4

Hence, $\lim\limits_{x \to 2} 4 = \lim\limits_{x \to 2} \dfrac{x^2 - 4}{x - 2} = 4$. Their limits give the same value of 4. This shows that f(x) exist, and that f(2) = $\lim\limits_{x \to 2}$ f(x). Therefore, the function is continuous.

Examples on Limits of Trigonometric Functions

1. Evaluate $\lim\limits_{x \to 0} \dfrac{\sin 2x}{5x}$

Solution

$$\lim\limits_{x \to 0} \dfrac{\sin 2x}{5x}$$

Substituting zero directly into the expression above will give $\dfrac{0}{0}$. Hence we have to apply the appropriate rule of limit. Let us first make an adjustment to the expression as follows.

Multiply the expression by $\dfrac{2x}{5x}$ and change the denominator to $2x$ just like the numerator, as follows:

$$\lim\limits_{x \to 0} \dfrac{\sin 2x}{5x} = \lim\limits_{x \to 0} \left(\dfrac{\sin 2x}{2x} \times \dfrac{2x}{5x}\right)$$

Note that when $2x$ cancels out, the original expression remains the same.

Recall that $\lim\limits_{x \to 0} \dfrac{\sin ax}{ax} = 1$

Hence, $\lim\limits_{x \to 0} \dfrac{\sin 2x}{2x} = 1$

Substituting 1 for $\lim\limits_{x \to 0} \dfrac{\sin 2x}{2x}$ in the simplification given above to gives:

$$\lim\limits_{x \to 0} \left(\dfrac{\sin 2x}{2x} \times \dfrac{2x}{5x}\right) = \lim\limits_{x \to 0} \dfrac{\sin 2x}{2x} \times \lim\limits_{x \to 0} \dfrac{2x}{5x}$$

$$= 1 \times \lim\limits_{x \to 0} \dfrac{2}{5} \quad (x \text{ cancels out})$$

$$= 1 \times \dfrac{2}{5} \quad (\text{Since } \lim\limits_{x \to a} c = c)$$

$$= \dfrac{2}{5}$$

2. 1. Evaluate $\lim\limits_{x \to 0} \dfrac{\sin 5x}{7x}$

Solution

$$\lim\limits_{x \to 0} \dfrac{\sin 5x}{7x}$$

Multiply the expression by $\frac{5x}{7x}$ and change the denominator to $5x$ just like the numerator. This gives:

$$\lim_{x \to 0} \frac{\sin 5x}{7x} = \lim_{x \to 0} \left(\frac{\sin 5x}{5x} \times \frac{5x}{7x} \right)$$

Hence, $\lim_{x \to 0} \frac{\sin 5x}{5x} = 1$

Substituting 1 for $\lim_{x \to 0} \frac{\sin 5x}{5x}$ in the simplification given above to gives:

$$\lim_{x \to 0} \left(\frac{\sin 5x}{5x} \times \frac{5x}{7x} \right) = \lim_{x \to 0} \frac{\sin 5x}{5x} \times \lim_{x \to 0} \frac{5x}{7x}$$

$$= 1 \times \lim_{x \to 0} \frac{5}{7} \quad (x \text{ cancels out})$$

$$= 1 \times \frac{5}{7} \quad \left(\text{Since } \lim_{x \to a} c = c \right)$$

$$= \frac{5}{7}$$

The two examples above show that $\lim_{x \to 0} \frac{\sin a\, x}{x} = a$ or $\lim_{x \to 0} \frac{\sin a\, x}{bx} = \frac{a}{b}$. This rule also applies to tangent as $\lim_{x \to 0} \frac{\tan a\, x}{x} = a$ or $\lim_{x \to 0} \frac{\tan a\, x}{bx} = \frac{a}{b}$.

3. Find the value of $\lim_{x \to \frac{\pi}{2}} \frac{\cos 2x}{\sin 3x}$

Solution

$$\lim_{x \to \frac{\pi}{2}} \frac{\cos 2x}{\sin 3x}$$

We can simply substitute in the value of x and obtain our answer.

$$\lim_{x \to \frac{\pi}{2}} \frac{\cos 2x}{\sin 3x} = \frac{\cos 2\left(\frac{\pi}{2}\right)}{\sin 3\left(\frac{\pi}{2}\right)}$$

$$= \frac{\cos \pi}{\sin \frac{3\pi}{2}}$$

$$= \frac{\cos 180}{\sin 270} \quad (\text{Note that } \pi \text{ radians} = 180^\circ)$$

$$= \frac{-1}{-1}$$

$$= 1$$

This problem can also be solved by using the angles directly in radians, but I prefer to work in degrees. Note that $\cos \pi$ in radians $= -1$, and $\sin \frac{3\pi}{2}$ in radians $= -1$ as obtained above.

4. Evaluate $\lim_{x \to 0} \frac{\cos x}{\sin x - 3}$

Solution

$$\lim_{x \to 0} \frac{\cos x}{\sin x - 3} = \frac{\cos 0}{\sin 0 - 3}$$

$$= \frac{1}{0 - 3}$$

$$= -\frac{1}{3}$$

5. Evaluate $\lim_{x \to 0} \dfrac{\sin 3x}{\sin 2x}$

<u>Solution</u>

Multiply by $\dfrac{x}{\sin 2x}$ and change the denominator to x as follows.

$$\lim_{x \to 0} \frac{\sin 3x}{\sin 2x} = \lim_{x \to 0} \left(\frac{\sin 3x}{x} \ \text{X} \ \frac{x}{\sin 2x} \right) \qquad \text{(When } x \text{ cancels out it gives the original expression)}$$

$$= \lim_{x \to 0} \left(\frac{\sin 3x}{x} \ \text{X} \ \left(\frac{\sin 2x}{x} \right)^{-1} \right) \qquad \text{(Note that the inverse of } \frac{x}{\sin 2x} \text{ has been taken)}$$

$$= \lim_{x \to 0} \frac{\sin 3x}{x} \ \text{X} \ \left(\lim_{x \to 0} \frac{\sin 2x}{x} \right)^{-1}$$

$$= 3 \ \text{x} \ 2^{-1} \qquad \text{(Note that } \lim_{x \to 0} \frac{\sin 3x}{x} = 3 \ \text{ and } \ \lim_{x \to 0} \frac{\sin 2x}{x} = 2\text{)}$$

$$= 3 \ \text{x} \ \frac{1}{2}$$

$$= \frac{3}{2}$$

This example shows that: $\lim_{x \to 0} \dfrac{\sin a x}{\sin b x} = \dfrac{a}{b}$

6. Evaluate $\lim_{x \to 0} \dfrac{\sin 2x}{\sin 5x}$

<u>Solution</u>

$$\lim_{x \to 0} \frac{\sin 2x}{\sin 5x}$$

From the rule established in example 5 above, we can see that the solution to this problem is $\dfrac{2}{5}$.

Hence, $\lim_{x \to 0} \dfrac{\sin 2x}{\sin 5x} = \dfrac{2}{5}$ \qquad (Since $\lim_{x \to 0} \dfrac{\sin a x}{\sin b x} = \dfrac{a}{b}$)

Exercise 1

1. Evaluate $\lim_{x \to 0} 2x^3 - 4x^2 + x + 9$

2. Evaluate $\lim_{x \to 0} \dfrac{5x^2 + x - 8}{x^2 - 2x + 5}$

3. Evaluate $\lim_{x \to 5} \dfrac{x^2 - x - 20}{x - 5}$

4. Evaluate $\lim\limits_{x\to 7} \dfrac{x^2-49}{x-7}$

5. Evaluate $\lim\limits_{x\to 0} (5x-1)(3x+7)(3x+2)$

6. Evaluate $\lim\limits_{x\to\infty} \dfrac{2x^3+x^2-9x-5}{5x^3+2x^2-7x+2}$

7. Evaluate $\lim\limits_{x\to\infty} \dfrac{x^4-5x^2-2x-6}{3x^4+2x+3}$

8. Evaluate $\lim\limits_{x\to 4} \dfrac{x^2-25}{x^2+2x-15}$

9. Evaluate $\lim\limits_{x\to 8} \dfrac{2x^2-17x+8}{8-x}$

10. Evaluate $\lim\limits_{m\to 0} \dfrac{(5+m)^2-25}{m}$

11. Determine the limiting value of $\dfrac{\sqrt{x}-2}{x-4}$ as x tends to 4 .

12. Find the limit of $\dfrac{x^3-27}{x-3}$ as $x \to 3$

13. Find the limit of $\dfrac{x^3+8}{x+2}$ as $x \to -2$

14. Evaluate $\lim\limits_{x\to 25} \dfrac{5-\sqrt{x}}{25-x}$

15. Evaluate $\lim\limits_{x\to 1} \dfrac{x^3-1}{x^7-1}$

16. Determine if the function $f(x) = x^2 + 3x - 1$ is continuous at the point $x = 2$

17. Determine if the function $f(x) = \dfrac{5x-2}{3x^2-x-2}$ is continuous at $x = -1$

18. Determine if the function $f(x) = \dfrac{2x^2-18}{x-3}$ is continuous at $x = 3$.

19. Determine if the function $f(x) = \dfrac{x^3+64}{x+4}$ is continuous at $x = -4$.

20. Test for the continuity of the function: $f(x) = \begin{cases} -x+5 & \text{if } x > 2 \\ x^3 + 10 & \text{if } x \le 2 \end{cases}$

21. Determine the continuity of the function: $f(x) = \begin{cases} 3x^2 & \text{if } x \ge -3 \\ x+30 & \text{if } x < -3 \end{cases}$

22. Determine if the function below is continuous or not.

$$f(x) = \begin{cases} \dfrac{x^2-25}{x+5} & \text{if } x \ge -5 \\ \dfrac{x+5}{2x+10} & \text{if } x < -5 \end{cases}$$

23. If $f(x) = \begin{cases} \dfrac{x^3-27}{x-3} \\ 1 \text{ if } x = 3 \end{cases}$ test for the continuity of the function at $x = 3$.

24. If $f(x) = \begin{cases} 2 - 3x & x < 1 \\ x^3 + 4 & x \geq 1 \end{cases}$ evaluate the following limits, if they exist.

(a) $\lim\limits_{x \to -2} f(x)$

(b) $\lim\limits_{x \to 1} f(x)$

25. Evaluate $\lim\limits_{x \to 2} (5 + |x - 2|)$ if it exists.

26. Evaluate $\lim\limits_{x \to 0} \dfrac{\sin 7x}{2x}$

27. Evaluate $\lim\limits_{x \to 0} \dfrac{\sin x}{3x}$

28. Find the value of $\lim\limits_{x \to \pi} \dfrac{\cos 2x}{\sin \frac{x}{2}}$

29. Evaluate $\lim\limits_{x \to 0} \dfrac{\cos 5x}{\sin 3x - 2}$

30. Evaluate $\lim\limits_{x \to 0} \dfrac{\sin 9x}{\sin 4x}$

CHAPTER 2
DIFFERENTIATION FROM FIRST PRINCIPLE

If y = f(x), then the gradient function of y or f(x) is given by:

$$g(x) = \frac{f(x + \Delta x) - f(x)}{\Delta x}$$

where Δx is the increment in x.

Applying limits has shown that as Δx tends to zero,

$$f'(x) = \lim_{\Delta x \to 0} \frac{f(x + \Delta x) - f(x)}{\Delta x}$$

$$\frac{dy}{dx} = \lim_{\Delta x \to 0} \frac{f(x + \Delta x) - f(x)}{\Delta x}$$

$\dfrac{dy}{dx}$ reads dee y dee x.

Note that f'(x) and $\dfrac{dy}{dx}$ can be interpreted as instantaneous rate of change of y with respect to x.

The technique of finding the derivative of a function by considering the limiting value is called differentiation from first principle.

Examples

1. Find the derivative of x from first principle.

Solution

Let, y = x

Increasing x by Δx will give an increase in y by Δy. This gives:

$\quad$ y + Δy = x + Δx

$\quad\quad$ Δy = x + Δx − y

$\quad\quad$ Δy = x + Δx − x $\quad$ (substitute x for y since y = x as given above from the question)

$\quad\quad$ Δy = Δx $\quad$ (x cancels out)

Dividing both sides by Δx in order to get the derivative gives:

$$\frac{\Delta y}{\Delta x} = \frac{\Delta x}{\Delta x}$$

$$\frac{\Delta y}{\Delta x} = 1$$

Taking limits as Δx tends to zero gives:

$\displaystyle\lim_{\Delta x \to 0} \frac{\Delta y}{\Delta x} = 1$ $\quad$ [Recall that $\displaystyle\lim_{x \to 0} c = c$, hence $\displaystyle\lim_{\Delta x \to 0} f(\Delta x) = 1$ gives 1, since $\dfrac{\Delta y}{\Delta x}$ is regarded as f(Δx)]

We now write $\displaystyle\lim_{\Delta x \to 0} \frac{\Delta y}{\Delta x}$ as $\dfrac{dy}{dx}$. This gives:

$$\frac{dy}{dx} = 1$$

2. Find from first principle, the derivative of $2x^3$.

<u>Solution</u>

Let, $y = 2x^3$

Increasing x by Δx will give an increase in y by Δy. This gives:

$$y + \Delta y = 2(x + \Delta x)^3$$
$$y + \Delta y = 2[x^3 + 3x^2\Delta x + 3x(\Delta x)^2 + (\Delta x)^3]$$
$$= 2x^3 + 6x^2\Delta x + 6x(\Delta x)^2 + 2(\Delta x)^3$$
$$\Delta y = 2x^3 + 6x^2\Delta x + 6x(\Delta x)^2 + 2(\Delta x)^3 - y$$
$$= 2x^3 + 6x^2\Delta x + 6x(\Delta x)^2 + 2(\Delta x)^3 - 2x^3 \quad \text{(Since } y = 2x^3\text{)}$$
$$\Delta y = 6x^2\Delta x + 6x(\Delta x)^2 + 2(\Delta x)^3 \quad \text{(Since } 2x^3 \text{ cancels out)}$$

Dividing both sides by Δx in order to get the derivative gives:

$$\frac{\Delta y}{\Delta x} = \frac{6x^2\Delta x}{\Delta x} + \frac{6x(\Delta x)^2}{\Delta x} + \frac{2(\Delta x)^3}{\Delta x}$$
$$\frac{\Delta y}{\Delta x} = 6x^2 + 6x\Delta x + 2(\Delta x)^2$$

Taking limits as Δx tends to zero gives:

$$\lim_{\Delta x \to 0} \frac{\Delta y}{\Delta x} = 6x^2 + 6x(0) + 2(0)^2 \quad \text{(Note that zero replaces } \Delta x\text{)}$$
$$\lim_{\Delta x \to 0} \frac{\Delta y}{\Delta x} = 6x^2$$

We now write $\lim_{\Delta x \to 0} \frac{\Delta y}{\Delta x}$ as $\frac{dy}{dx}$. This gives:

$$\frac{dy}{dx} = 6x^2$$

3. Find the derivative of $f(x) = \dfrac{1}{x^2}$ from first principle.

<u>Solution</u>

$$f(x) = \Delta x$$

Increasing x by Δx gives:

$$f(x + \Delta x) = \frac{1}{(x + \Delta x)^2}$$
$$f(x + \Delta x) = \frac{1}{x^2 + 2x\Delta x + (\Delta x)^2}$$

Subtract $f(x)$ from both sides of the equation

$$f(x + \Delta x) - f(x) = \frac{1}{x^2 + 2x\Delta x + (\Delta x)^2} - f(x)$$
$$f(x + \Delta x) - f(x) = \frac{1}{x^2 + 2x\Delta x + (\Delta x)^2} - \frac{1}{x^2} \quad \text{(Note that } f(x) = \frac{1}{x^2}\text{)}$$
$$= \frac{x^2 - (x^2 + 2x\Delta x + (\Delta x)^2)}{x^2(x^2 + 2x\Delta x + (\Delta x)^2)}$$
$$= \frac{x^2 - x^2 - 2x\Delta x - (\Delta x)^2}{x^2(x^2 + 2x\Delta x + (\Delta x)^2)}$$

$$= \frac{-2x\Delta x - (\Delta x)^2}{x^2(x^2 + 2x\Delta x + (\Delta x)^2)}$$

$$f(x + \Delta x) - f(x) = \frac{\Delta x(-2x - \Delta x)}{x^2(x^2 + 2x\Delta x + (\Delta x)^2)}$$

Dividing both sides by Δx gives:

$$\frac{f(x + \Delta x) - f(x)}{\Delta x} = \frac{-2x - \Delta x}{x^2(x^2 + 2x\Delta x + (\Delta x)^2)}$$ (Δx has cancelled out from the right hand side)

Taking limits as Δx tends to zero gives:

$$\lim_{\Delta x \to 0} \frac{f(x + \Delta x) - f(x)}{\Delta x} = \frac{-2x - 0}{x^2(x^2 + 2x(0) + (0)^2)}$$

Replacing $\displaystyle\lim_{\Delta x \to 0} \frac{f(x + \Delta x) - f(x)}{\Delta x}$ with f'(x) gives the derivative of f(x) as:

$$f'(x) = \frac{-2x}{x^2(x^2)}$$

$$f'(x) = \frac{-2}{x^3}$$

4. If $f(x) = 3x^2$

(a) write down and simplify the expression $\dfrac{f(x + h) - f(x)}{h}$ (h $\neq$ 0)

(b) find $\displaystyle\lim_{\Delta x \to 0} \frac{f(x + h) - f(x)}{h}$

Solution

(a) Let, $f(x) = 3x^2$

Increasing x by h gives:

$$f(x + h) = 3(x + h)^2$$
$$= 3[x^2 + 2xh + h^2]$$
$$= 3x^2 + 6xh + 3h^2$$

Subtracting f(x) from both sides gives:

$$f(x + h) - f(x) = 3x^2 + 6xh + 3h^2 - 3x^2$$ (Note that $f(x) = 3x^2$ from the question)
$$= 6xh + 3h^2$$

Dividing both side by h gives:

$$\frac{f(x + h) - f(x)}{h} = \frac{6xh}{h} + \frac{3h^2}{h}$$

$$\frac{f(x + h) - f(x)}{h} = 6x + 3h$$

(b) $\dfrac{f(x + h) - f(x)}{h} = 6x + 3h$

Taking limits as h tends to zero gives:

$$\lim_{h \to 0} \frac{f(x + h) - f(x)}{h} = 6x + 3(0)$$

$$\lim_{h \to 0} \frac{f(x + h) - f(x)}{h} = 6x$$

23

5. If $f(x) = 4x^3 - 5$,

(a) evaluate $\dfrac{f(x+h) - f(x)}{h}$, where $h \neq 0$

(b) From your result in (5a) above , find the derivatives of $f(x)$ with respect to x.

Solution

(a) Let, $f(x) = 4x^3 - 5$

Increasing x by h gives:

$$f(x + h) = 4(x + h)^3 - 5$$
$$= 4[x^3 + 3x^2h + 3xh^2 + h^3] - 5$$
$$= 4x^3 + 12x^2h + 12xh^2 + 4h^3 - 5$$

Subtracting $f(x)$ from both sides gives:

$$f(x + h) - f(x) = 4x^3 + 12x^2h + 12xh^2 + 4h^3 - 5 - (4x^3 - 5) \quad (f(x) = 4x^3 - 5 \text{ from the question})$$
$$= 4x^3 + 12x^2h + 12xh^2 + 4h^3 - 5 - 4x^3 + 5$$
$$= 12x^2h + 12xh^2 + 4h^3$$

Dividing both side by h gives:

$$\frac{f(x+h) - f(x)}{h} = 12x^2 + 12xh + 4h^2$$

(b) $\dfrac{f(x+h) - f(x)}{h} = 12x^2 + 12xh + 4h^2$

Taking limits as h tends to zero gives:

$$\lim_{h \to 0} \frac{f(x+h) - f(x)}{h} = 12x^2 + 12x(0) \ 4(0)^2$$

$$\lim_{h \to 0} \frac{f(x+h) - f(x)}{h} = 12x^2$$

6. If $f(x) = \dfrac{x^2 + 1}{2x}$

(a) write down and simplify the expression $\dfrac{f(x + \Delta x) - f(\Delta x)}{\Delta x}$, where $\Delta x \neq 0$

(b) Find the derivatives of $y = \dfrac{x^2 + 1}{2x}$

Solution

$$f(x) = \frac{x^2 + 1}{2x}$$

$$f(x + \Delta x) = \frac{(x + \Delta x)^2 + 1}{2(x + \Delta x)}$$

$$f(x + \Delta x) = \frac{x^2 + 2x\Delta x + (\Delta x)^2 + 1}{2x + 2\Delta x}$$

Subtract $f(x)$ from both sides of the equation

$$f(x + \Delta x) - f(x) = \frac{x^2 + 2x\Delta x + (\Delta x)^2 + 1}{2x + 2\Delta x} - \frac{x^2 + 1}{2x}$$

$$f(x + \Delta x) - f(x) = \frac{2x[x^2 + 2x\Delta x + (\Delta x)^2 + 1] - (x^2 + 1)(2x + 2\Delta x)}{2x(2x + 2\Delta x)}$$

$$= \frac{2x^3 + 4x^2\Delta x + 2x(\Delta x)^2 + 2x - (2x^3 + 2x^2\Delta x + 2x + 2\Delta x)}{2x(2x + 2\Delta x)}$$

$$= \frac{2x^3 + 4x^2\Delta x + 2x(\Delta x)^2 + 2x - 2x^3 - 2x^2\Delta x - 2x - 2\Delta x)}{2x(2x + 2\Delta x)}$$

$$= \frac{2x^2\Delta x + 2x(\Delta x)^2 - 2\Delta x)}{2x(2x + 2\Delta x)}$$

$$f(x + \Delta x) - f(x) = \frac{\Delta x(2x^2 + 2x\Delta x - 2)}{2x(2x + 2\Delta x)} \qquad \text{(After factorizing the numerator)}$$

Dividing both sides by Δx gives:

$$\frac{f(x + \Delta x) - f(x)}{\Delta x} = \frac{2x^2 + 2x\Delta x - 2}{2x(2x + 2\Delta x)}$$

(b)Taking limits as Δx tends to zero gives:

$$\lim_{\Delta x \to 0} \frac{f(x + \Delta x) - f(x)}{\Delta x} = \frac{2x^2 + 2x(0) - 2}{2x(2x + 2(0))}$$

$$= \frac{2x^2 - 2}{2x(2x)}$$

$$= \frac{2(x^2 - 1)}{4x^2}$$

Replacing $\lim_{\Delta x \to 0} \frac{f(x + \Delta x) - f(x)}{\Delta x}$ with f'(x) gives the derivative of f(x) as:

$$f'(x) = \frac{x^2 - 1}{2x^2}$$

Separating into fractions gives:

$$f'(x) = \frac{x^2}{2x^2} - \frac{1}{2x^2}$$

$$f'(x) = \frac{1}{2} - \frac{1}{2x^2}$$

7. Find from first principle the derivatives with respect to x of y = $5x^3 - x + 7$

<u>Solution</u>

$$y = 5x^3 - x + 7$$

$$y + \Delta y = 5(x + \Delta x)^3 - (x + \Delta x) + 7$$

$$y + \Delta y = 5[x^3 + 3x^2\Delta x + 3x(\Delta x)^2 + (\Delta x)^3] - x - \Delta x + 7$$

$$= 5x^3 + 15x^2\Delta x + 15x(\Delta x)^2 + 5(\Delta x)^3 - x - \Delta x + 7$$

$$\Delta y = 5x^3 + 15x^2\Delta x + 15x(\Delta x)^2 + 5(\Delta x)^3 - x - \Delta x + 7 - y$$

$$= 5x^3 + 15x^2\Delta x + 15x(\Delta x)^2 + 5(\Delta x)^3 - x - \Delta x + 7 - (5x^3 - x + 7) \quad \text{(Since y = } 5x^3 - x + 7)$$

$$\Delta y = 5x^3 + 15x^2\Delta x + 15x(\Delta x)^2 + 5(\Delta x)^3 - x - \Delta x + 7 - 5x^3 + x - 7$$

25

$$= 15x^2\Delta x + 15x(\Delta x)^2 + 5(\Delta x)^3 - \Delta x$$

Dividing both sides by Δx gives:

$$\frac{\Delta y}{\Delta x} = \frac{15x^2\Delta x}{\Delta x} + \frac{15x(\Delta x)^2}{\Delta x} + \frac{5(\Delta x)^3}{\Delta x} - \frac{\Delta x}{\Delta x}$$

$$\frac{\Delta y}{\Delta x} = 15x^2 + 15x\Delta x + 5(\Delta x)^2 - 1$$

Taking limits as Δx tends to zero gives:

$$\lim_{\Delta x \to 0} \frac{\Delta y}{\Delta x} = 15x^2 + 15x(0) + 5(0)^2 - 1$$

$$\lim_{\Delta x \to 0} \frac{\Delta y}{\Delta x} = 15x^2 - 1$$

We now replace $\lim_{\Delta x \to 0} \frac{\Delta y}{\Delta x}$ with $\frac{dy}{dx}$. This gives:

$$\frac{dy}{dx} = 15x^2 - 1$$

8. Differentiate $3x - \dfrac{1}{2x^2}$ from first principle.

<u>Solution</u>

$$y = 3x - \frac{1}{x^2}$$

$$y + \Delta y = 3(x + \Delta x) - \frac{1}{2(x + \Delta x)^2}$$

$$= 3x + 3\Delta x - \frac{1}{2[x^2 + 2x\Delta x + (\Delta x)^2]}$$

Subtract y from both sides of the equation

$$\Delta y = 3x + 3\Delta x - \frac{1}{2x^2 + 4x\Delta x + 2(\Delta x)^2} - y$$

$$= 3x + 3\Delta x - \frac{1}{2x^2 + 4x\Delta x + 2(\Delta x)^2} - \left(3x - \frac{1}{2x^2}\right)$$

$$= 3x + 3\Delta x - \frac{1}{2x^2 + 4x\Delta x + 2(\Delta x)^2} - 3x + \frac{1}{2x^2}$$

$$= 3\Delta x - \frac{1}{2x^2 + 4x\Delta x + 2(\Delta x)^2} + \frac{1}{2x^2}$$

Combining them into one fraction gives:

$$\Delta y = \frac{3\Delta x[2x^2(2x^2 + 4x\Delta x + 2(\Delta x)^2] - 2x^2 + 2x^2 + 4x\Delta x + 2(\Delta x)^2}{2x^2[2x^2 + 4x\Delta x + 2(\Delta x)^2]}$$

$$= \frac{3\Delta x[4x^4 + 8x^3\Delta x + 4x^2(\Delta x)^2] + 4x\Delta x + 2(\Delta x)^2}{2x^2[2x^2 + 4x\Delta x + 2(\Delta x)^2]} \quad (-2x^2 + 2x^2 \text{ has cancelled out})$$

$$= \frac{12x^4\Delta x + 24x^3(\Delta x)^2 + 12x^2(\Delta x)^3 + 4x\Delta x + 2(\Delta x)^2}{2x^2[2x^2 + 4x\Delta x + 2(\Delta x)^2]}$$

Factorizing the numerator gives:

$$= \frac{\Delta x[12x^4 + 24x^3\Delta x + 12x^2(\Delta x)^2 + 4x + 2\Delta x]}{2x^2[2x^2 + 4x\Delta x + 2(\Delta x)^2]}$$

26

Dividing both sides by Δx gives:

$$\frac{\Delta y}{\Delta x} = \frac{12x^4 + 24x^3\Delta x + 12x^2(\Delta x)^2 + 4x + 2\Delta x}{2x^2[2x^2 + 4x\Delta x + 2(\Delta x)^2]} \quad (\Delta x \text{ that is outside the bracket cancels out})$$

Taking limits as Δx tends to zero gives:

$$\lim_{\Delta x \to 0} \frac{\Delta y}{\Delta x} = \frac{12x^4 + 24x^3(0) + 12x^2(0)^2 + 4x + 2(0)}{2x^2[2x^2 + 4x(0) + 2(0)^2]}$$

$$= \frac{12x^4 + 4x}{2x^2[2x^2]}$$

$$\lim_{\Delta x \to 0} \frac{\Delta y}{\Delta x} = \frac{12x^4 + 4x}{4x^4}$$

$$= \frac{12x^4}{4x^4} + \frac{4x}{4x^4}$$

$$= 3 + \frac{1}{x^3}$$

Replacing $\lim_{\Delta x \to 0} \frac{\Delta y}{\Delta x}$ with $\frac{dy}{dx}$ gives the derivative as:

$$\frac{dy}{dx} = 3 + \frac{1}{x^3}$$

Exercise 2

1. Find the derivative of $2x$ from first principle.

2. Find from first principle, the derivative of x^2.

3. Find the derivative of $f(x) = \dfrac{1}{x^3}$ from first principle.

4. If $f(x) = 5x^2$

(a) write down and simplify the expression $\dfrac{f(x+h) - f(x)}{h}$ $\quad (h \neq 0)$

(b) find $\lim_{h \to 0} \dfrac{f(x+h) - f(x)}{h}$

5. If $f(x) = 9x^3$,

(a) evaluate $\dfrac{f(x+h) - f(x)}{h}$, where $h \neq 0$

(b) From your result above, find the derivatives of $f(x)$ with respect to x.

6. If $f(x) = \dfrac{x^3 - 2}{x}$

(a) write down and simplify the expression $\dfrac{f(x + \Delta x) - f(\Delta x)}{\Delta x}$, where $\Delta x \neq 0$

(b) Find the derivatives of $y = \dfrac{x^3 - 2}{x}$

7. Find from first principle the derivatives with respect to x of $y = 3x^2 - 10x$

8. Differentiate $x + \dfrac{3}{x}$ from first principle.

9. From first principle, find the derivatives with respect to x of $y = 5x - 3x^2$

10. Differentiate $2x + \dfrac{x}{5}$ from first principle.

CHAPTER 3
GENERAL RULE OF DIFFERENTIATION AND COMPOSITE FUNCTIONS

The general rule for the derivative/differentiation of a function is as given below.

If $y = x^n$

then, $\dfrac{dy}{dx} = nx^{n-1}$

The rule for differentiating a composite function (or function of a function) is given as follows:

If $y = (2x + 5)^4$

then we write, $u = 2x + 5$

and express y as:

$y = u^4$

Therefore, $\dfrac{dy}{dx} = \dfrac{dy}{du} \times \dfrac{du}{dx}$

This rule is called the chain rule.

Examples

1. Find the derivatives of the following:

(a) $y = 2x^7$

(b) $y = \dfrac{3}{4}x^8$

(c) $y = 3\sqrt{x}$

(d) $y = \dfrac{10}{\sqrt[5]{x^3}}$

(e) $y = \dfrac{1}{x^{\frac{1}{4}}}$

Solution

(a) $y = 2x^7$

Solutions

(a) $y = 2x^7$

$\dfrac{dy}{dx} = 7 \times 2x^{7-1}$

This is done by multiplying the exponent (power) by the term and subtracting 1 from the exponent (power). Hence, the answer is:

$\dfrac{dy}{dx} = 14x^6$

(b) $y = \dfrac{3}{4}x^8$

Multiply the term by the exponent (power) (i.e. 8) and subtract 1 from the exponent. This gives:

$\dfrac{dy}{dx} = 8 \times \dfrac{3}{4}x^{8-1}$

$$= \frac{24}{4} x^7$$

$$\frac{dy}{dx} = 6x^7$$

(c) $y = 3\sqrt{x}$

Since $\sqrt{x} = x^{\frac{1}{2}}$, we can rewrite the expression as:

$$y = 3x^{\frac{1}{2}}$$

$$\frac{dy}{dx} = \frac{1}{2} \times 3x^{\frac{1}{2} - 1}$$

$$= \frac{3}{2} x^{-\frac{1}{2}}$$

$$= \frac{3}{2} \times \frac{1}{x^{\frac{1}{2}}} \qquad \text{(Note that } x^{-\frac{1}{2}} = \frac{1}{x^{\frac{1}{2}}} \text{ from indices)}$$

$$\frac{dy}{dx} = \frac{3}{2x^{\frac{1}{2}}}$$

$$\frac{dy}{dx} = \frac{3}{2\sqrt{x}} \qquad \text{(Since } x^{\frac{1}{2}} = \sqrt{x} \text{)}$$

(d) $y = \dfrac{10}{\sqrt[5]{x^3}}$

Expressing the root in fractional form gives:

$$y = \frac{10}{(x^3)^{\frac{1}{5}}}$$

$$y = \frac{10}{x^{\frac{3}{5}}} \qquad \text{(The two exponents (powers) 3 and } \frac{1}{5} \text{ have been multiplied)}$$

Taking the denominator to the numerator changes the sign of its exponent as follows:

$$y = 10x^{-\frac{3}{5}}$$

Hence, $\dfrac{dy}{dx} = -\dfrac{3}{5} \times 10x^{-\frac{3}{5} - 1}$

$$= -\frac{30}{5} x^{-\frac{8}{5}}$$

$$= -6 x^{-\frac{8}{5}}$$

$$= -6 \times \frac{1}{x^{\frac{8}{5}}} \qquad \text{(Note that the inverse of a term changes the sign of its exponent)}$$

$$\frac{dy}{dx} = \frac{-6}{x^{\frac{8}{5}}}$$

Or, $\dfrac{dy}{dx} = \dfrac{-6}{\sqrt[5]{x^8}}$

(e) $y = \dfrac{1}{x^{\frac{1}{4}}}$

This can be expressed as:

$y = x^{-\frac{1}{4}}$

$\dfrac{dy}{dx} = -\dfrac{1}{4}x^{-\frac{1}{4}-1}$

$= -\dfrac{1}{4}x^{-\frac{5}{4}}$

$= -\dfrac{1}{4} \times \dfrac{1}{x^{\frac{5}{4}}}$

$\dfrac{dy}{dx} = -\dfrac{1}{4x^{\frac{5}{4}}}$ (Note that the inverse of a term changes the sign of its exponent)

Or, $\dfrac{dy}{dx} = \dfrac{1}{4\sqrt[4]{x^5}}$

2. Find the derivative of each of the following:

(a) $5x^3 - 7x^2 - 3x + 8$

(b) $\dfrac{3}{5}x^5 + 2x^3 - x$

(c) $\dfrac{2x^4 - 5x^3 - 4x^2 + 3}{x^2}$

(d) $\sqrt{x} + \dfrac{1}{\sqrt{x}}$

Solutions

(a) Let the expression be $y = 5x^3 - 7x^2 - 3x + 8$

Hence, $\dfrac{dy}{dx} = \dfrac{d(5x^3)}{dx} - \dfrac{d(7x^2)}{dx} - \dfrac{d(3x)}{dx} + \dfrac{d(8)}{dx}$

This means that each part should be differentiated separately.

Hence, $\dfrac{dy}{dx} = (3 \times 5x^{3-1}) - (2 \times 7x^{2-1}) - (1 \times 3x^{1-1}) + 0$

$\dfrac{dy}{dx} = 15x^2 - 14x - 3$ (Note that $x^0 = 1$)

Note that the derivative of a constant is zero as shown by the derivative of 8

(b) $y = \dfrac{3}{5}x^5 + 2x^3 - x$

$\qquad \dfrac{dy}{dx} = \left(5 \times \dfrac{3}{5}x^{5-1}\right) + \left(3 \times 2x^{3-1}\right) - \left(1 \times x^{1-1}\right)$

$\qquad \qquad = 3x^4 + 6x^2 - 1$

(c) $y = \dfrac{2x^4 - 5x^3 - 4x^2 + 3}{x^2}$

Dividing each term in the numerator by the denominator in order to separate the expression into it different fractions gives:

$\qquad y = \dfrac{2x^4}{x^2} - \dfrac{5x^3}{x^2} - \dfrac{4x^2}{x^2} + \dfrac{3}{x^2}$

$\qquad \qquad = 2x^2 - 5x - 4 + \dfrac{3}{x^2}$

$\qquad y = 2x^2 - 5x - 4 + 3x^{-2}$

$\qquad \dfrac{dy}{dx} = (2 \times 2x) - 5 - 0 + \left(-2 \times 3x^{-2-1}\right)$

$\qquad \qquad = 4x - 5 - 6x^{-3}$

$\qquad \dfrac{dy}{dx} = 4x - 5 - \dfrac{6}{x^2}$

(d) $y = \sqrt{x} + \dfrac{1}{\sqrt{x}}$

$\qquad = x^{\frac{1}{2}} + \dfrac{1}{x^{\frac{1}{2}}}$

$\qquad y = x^{\frac{1}{2}} + x^{-\frac{1}{2}}$

$\qquad \dfrac{dy}{dx} = \dfrac{1}{2}x^{-\frac{1}{2}} - \dfrac{1}{2}x^{-\frac{3}{2}}$ $\qquad$ (Note that $-\dfrac{1}{2} - 1 = -\dfrac{3}{2}$)

$\qquad \qquad = \dfrac{1}{2} \times \dfrac{1}{x^{\frac{1}{2}}} - \dfrac{1}{2} \times \dfrac{1}{x^{\frac{3}{2}}}$

$\qquad \qquad = \dfrac{1}{2x^{\frac{1}{2}}} - \dfrac{1}{2x^{\frac{3}{2}}}$

$\qquad \dfrac{dy}{dx} = \dfrac{1}{2\sqrt{x}} - \dfrac{1}{2\sqrt{x^3}}$

3. If $y = (5x - 2)^3$, find $\dfrac{dy}{dx}$

Solution

$\qquad y = (5x - 2)^3$ $\qquad$ (This is a composite function)

Let us take u = 5x – 2

If 5x – 2 is replaced with U, then the question (i.e. y = (5x – 2)^3) becomes:

$$y = u^3$$

Hence, $\dfrac{dy}{du} = 3u^2$

Since u = 5x – 2

then $\dfrac{du}{dx} = 5$

Therefore, $\dfrac{dy}{dx} = \dfrac{dy}{du}$ x $\dfrac{du}{dx}$ (Chain rule)

$$= 3u^2 \text{ x } 5$$

$$= 15u^2$$

Now substitute 5x – 2 for u to obtain $\dfrac{dy}{dx}$ as follows:

$$\dfrac{dy}{dx} = 15(5x – 2)^2$$

4. If y = $\dfrac{1}{(5x^2 – 1)^4}$ find $\dfrac{dy}{dx}$

Solution

$$y = \dfrac{1}{(5x^2 – 1)^4}$$ (This is a composite function)

It can also be represented as follows:

y = $(5x^2 – 1)^{-4}$ (Its inverse changes the sign of its exponent)

Now, let us take u = 5x^2 – 1

Hence, y = u^{-4} (When 5x^2 – 1 is replaced with u in the original question)

Therefore, $\dfrac{dy}{du} = -4u^{-5}$

Since u = 5x^2 – 1

then, $\dfrac{du}{dx} = 10x$

Therefore, $\dfrac{dy}{dx} = \dfrac{dy}{du}$ x $\dfrac{du}{dx}$ (Chain rule)

$$= -4u^{-5} \text{ x } 10x$$

$$\dfrac{dy}{dx} = -40xu^{-5}$$

Now substitute 5x^2 – 1 for u. This gives:

$$\dfrac{dy}{dx} = -40x(5x^2 – 1)^{-5}$$

Or, $\dfrac{dy}{dx} = \dfrac{-40x}{(5x^2 – 1)^5}$ (Note the change in the sign of the exponent as it becomes

denominator)

5. If $y = (2x^3 + 7x)^{\frac{1}{2}}$ find $\dfrac{dy}{dx}$

Solution

$$y = (2x^3 + 7x)^{\frac{1}{2}}$$

Let $u = 2x^3 + 7x$

Hence, $y = u^{\frac{1}{2}}$

$$\frac{dy}{du} = \frac{1}{2} u^{-\frac{1}{2}}$$

Also, $u = 2x^3 + 7x$

$$\frac{du}{dx} = 6x^2 + 7$$

Therefore, $\dfrac{dy}{dx} = \dfrac{dy}{du} \times \dfrac{du}{dx}$

$$= \frac{1}{2} u^{-\frac{1}{2}} \times 6x^2 + 7$$

$$= \frac{6x^2 + 7}{2} u^{-\frac{1}{2}}$$

$$= \frac{6x^2 + 7}{2} \times \frac{1}{u^{1/2}}$$

$$\frac{dy}{dx} = \frac{6x^2 + 7}{2u^{1/2}}$$

Now, replace u with $2x^3 + 7x$. This gives:

$$\frac{dy}{dx} = \frac{6x^2 + 7}{2(2x^3 + 7x)^{1/2}}$$

Or, $\dfrac{dy}{dx} = \dfrac{6x^2 + 7}{2\sqrt{2x^3 + 7x}}$ (Note that $(2x^3 + 7x)^{\frac{1}{2}} = \sqrt{2x^3 + 7x}$)

6. Find the derivative of $3x^2 - x + 9)^4$

Solution

$$y = (3x^2 - x + 9)^4$$

Let $u = 3x^2 - x + 9$

Hence, $y = u^4$

$$\frac{dy}{du} = 4u^3$$

$$\frac{du}{dx} = 6x - 1$$

Therefore, $\dfrac{dy}{dx} = \dfrac{dy}{du} \times \dfrac{du}{dx}$

$$= 4u^3 \times 6x - 1$$

$$= 4(6x - 1)u^3$$

$$= (24x - 4)u^3$$

$$\frac{dy}{dx} = (24x - 4)(3x^2 - x + 9)^3 \qquad \text{(When u is replaced with } 3x^2 - x + 9)$$

7. Find the derivative of $\left(x - \dfrac{5}{x}\right)^4$

Solution

$$y = \left(x - \frac{5}{x}\right)^4$$

Let $u = x - \dfrac{5}{x}$

Therefore, $y = u^4$

$$\frac{dy}{du} = 4u^3$$

$$\frac{du}{dx} = \frac{d(x)}{dx} - \frac{d(5x^{-1})}{dx} \qquad \text{(Note that} = \frac{5}{x} = 5x^{-1})$$

$$= 1 - (-1)5x^{-2}$$

$$= 1 + 5x^{-2}$$

$$\frac{du}{dx} = 1 + \frac{5}{x^2}$$

Therefore, $\dfrac{dy}{dx} = \dfrac{dy}{du} \times \dfrac{du}{dx}$

$$= 4u^3 \times \left(1 + \frac{5}{x^2}\right)$$

$$= \left(4 + \frac{20}{x^2}\right)u^3$$

$$\frac{dy}{dx} = \left(4 + \frac{20}{x^2}\right)\left(x - \frac{5}{x}\right)^3 \qquad \text{(When u is replaced with } \left(x - \frac{5}{x}\right))$$

8. Differentiate with respect to x: $\dfrac{1}{2x^5 - 3x + 1}$

Solution

Let $y = \dfrac{1}{2x^5 - 3x + 1}$

Or, $y = (2x^5 - 3x + 1)^{-1} \qquad \text{(Recall from indices that } \frac{1}{a} = a^{-1})$

Let us take $u = 2x^5 - 3x + 1$

Therefore, $y = u^{-1}$

$$\frac{dy}{du} = -1u^{-2}$$

$$\frac{du}{dx} = 10x^4 - 3$$

Therefore, $\dfrac{dy}{dx} = \dfrac{dy}{du} \times \dfrac{du}{dx}$

$$= -1u^{-2} \times 10x^4 - 3$$

$$= -1(10x^4 - 3)u^{-2}$$

$$= (-10x^4 + 3)u^{-2}$$

$$= \frac{3 - 10x^4}{u^2}$$

$$\frac{dy}{dx} = \frac{3 - 10x^4}{(2x^5 - 3x + 1)^2}$$

9. Differentiate with respect to x: $\sqrt{7 - 5x^3}$

Solution

Let $y = \sqrt{7 - 5x^3}$

Or, $y = (7 - 5x^3)^{\frac{1}{2}}$ (Recall from indices that $\sqrt{a} = a^{\frac{1}{2}}$)

Let $u = 7 - 5x^3$

Hence, $y = u^{\frac{1}{2}}$

$$\frac{dy}{du} = \frac{1}{2}u^{-\frac{1}{2}}$$

$$\frac{du}{dx} = -15x^2$$

Therefore, $\dfrac{dy}{dx} = \dfrac{dy}{du} \times \dfrac{du}{dx}$

$$= \frac{1}{2}u^{-\frac{1}{2}} \times (-15x^2)$$

$$= -\frac{15}{2}x^2 (u^{-\frac{1}{2}})$$

$$= -\frac{15x^2}{2u^{\frac{1}{2}}}$$

$$= -\frac{15x^2}{2\sqrt{u}}$$

$$\frac{dy}{dx} = -\frac{15x^2}{2\sqrt{7 - 5x^3}}$$

10. Find $\dfrac{dy}{dx}$ if $y = \dfrac{1}{\sqrt{2x^3 - 5}}$

Solution

$$y = \frac{1}{\sqrt{2x^3 - 5}}$$

Let $u = 2x^3 - 5$

hence, $y = \dfrac{1}{\sqrt{u}}$

$$y = \frac{1}{u^{\frac{1}{2}}}$$

$$y = u^{-\frac{1}{2}}$$

$$\frac{dy}{du} = -\frac{1}{2}u^{-\frac{3}{2}}$$ (Note that $-\frac{1}{2} - 1 = -\frac{3}{2}$)

36

$$\frac{du}{dx} = 6x^2$$

Therefore, $\dfrac{dy}{dx} = \dfrac{dy}{du} \times \dfrac{du}{dx}$

$$= -\frac{1}{2}u^{-\frac{3}{2}} \times (6x^2)$$

$$= -\frac{6}{2}x^2\,(u^{-\frac{3}{2}})$$

$$= -3x^2(u^{-\frac{3}{2}})$$

$$= -\frac{3x^2}{u^{\frac{3}{2}}}$$

$$= -\frac{3x^2}{\sqrt{u^3}}$$

$$\frac{dy}{dx} = -\frac{3x^2}{\sqrt{(2x^3 - 5)^3}}$$

Exercise 3

1. Find the derivatives of the following:

(a) $y = 8x^5$

(b) $y = \dfrac{2}{5}x^5$

(c) $y = \sqrt[3]{x}$

(d) $y = 7\sqrt[7]{x}$

(e) $y = \dfrac{1}{\sqrt[8]{x^5}}$

(f) $y = \dfrac{2}{x^{\frac{5}{2}}}$

2. Find the derivative of each of the following:

(a) $2x^5 - 3x^4 - 4x^3 + 5x^2 - 6x + 7$

(b) $x^7 + 2x^4 - \dfrac{3}{x}$

(c) $\dfrac{3x^9 - x^7 - 5x^4 + 2x^2 - 1}{x^3}$

(d) $5(\sqrt[4]{x}) + \dfrac{5}{\sqrt[3]{2x}}$

3. If $y = (2x - 5)^4$, find $\dfrac{dy}{dx}$

4. If $y = \dfrac{3}{(x^3 - 7)^2}$ find $\dfrac{dy}{dx}$

5. If $y = (2x^3 + 7x)^{\frac{1}{2}}$ find $\dfrac{dy}{dx}$

6. Find the derivative of $(7x^3 - x^2 + 3)^5$

7. Find the derivative of $\left(3x - \dfrac{2}{3x}\right)^3$

8. Differentiate with respect to x: $\quad -\dfrac{9}{3x^2 - x - 10}$

9. Differentiate with respect to x: $\quad \sqrt{1 - 2x^4}$

10. Find $\dfrac{dy}{dx}$ if $y = \dfrac{1}{\sqrt[3]{5x^3 - 1}}$

11. Find the derivative of $(x^5 - 3)^9$

12. Find the derivative of $\left(x - \dfrac{1}{5x}\right)^2$

13. Differentiate with respect to x: $\quad \dfrac{2}{x^3 - x - \frac{1}{x}}$

14. Differentiate with respect to x: $\quad \sqrt{5x - x^2}$

15. Find $\dfrac{dy}{dx}$ if $y = \dfrac{1}{\sqrt[5]{x^3 + 2}}$

CHAPTER 4
PRODUCT RULE OF DERIVATIVE

If $y = uv$ where u and v are functions of x, then:

$$\frac{dy}{dx} = u\frac{dv}{dx} + v\frac{du}{dx}$$

This is called the product rule of differentiation.

Similarly, If $y = uvw$ where u, v and w are functions of x, then:

$$\frac{dy}{dx} = \frac{du}{dx}vw + \frac{dv}{dx}uw + \frac{dw}{dx}uv$$

Examples

1. If $f(x) = (x - 3)(x + 4)$, find $f'(x)$

Solution

$$f(x) = (x - 3)(x + 4)$$

This is a product of two functions of x.

Let $u = x - 3$

and $v = x + 4$

Hence, $\dfrac{du}{dx} = 1$

$\dfrac{dv}{dx} = 1$

Therefore, the derivative of $f(x)$ is:

$$f'(x) = u\frac{dv}{dx} + v\frac{du}{dx}$$
$$= (x - 3) \times 1 + (x + 4) \times 1$$
$$= x - 3 + x + 4$$
$$f'(x) = 2x + 1$$

Note that another way to differentiate the function in example 1 above is to expand the bracket and differentiate directly.

2. Find the derivative of $y = (4x^2 + 1)(x^2 - 3)$

Solution

$$y = (4x^2 + 1)(x^2 - 3)$$

Let $u = 4x^2 + 1$

and $v = (x^2 - 3)$

Hence, $\dfrac{du}{dx} = 8x$

$\dfrac{dv}{dx} = 2x$

$$\frac{dy}{dx} = u\frac{dv}{dx} + v\frac{du}{dx}$$
$$= (4x^2 + 1)2x + (x^2 - 3)8x$$
$$= 8x^3 + 2x + 8x^3 - 24x$$
$$\frac{dy}{dx} = 16x^3 - 22x$$

3. If $y = x^2(1 + 2x)^{\frac{1}{2}}$, find $\frac{dy}{dx}$

Solution

$$y = x^2(1 + 2x)^{\frac{1}{2}}$$
$$u = x^2$$

and $v = (1 + 2x)^{\frac{1}{2}}$

Hence, $\frac{du}{dx} = 2x$

$$\frac{dv}{dx} = \frac{1}{2} \times 2 \times (1 + 2x)^{\frac{1}{2} - 1} \qquad \text{(Use of chain rule)}$$
$$= (1 + 2x)^{-\frac{1}{2}}$$
$$\frac{dv}{dx} = \frac{1}{(1+2x)^{\frac{1}{2}}}$$

Hence, $\frac{dy}{dx} = u\frac{dv}{dx} + v\frac{du}{dx}$

$$= x^2 \frac{1}{(1+2x)^{\frac{1}{2}}} + (1 + 2x)^{\frac{1}{2}} \times 2x$$
$$= \frac{x^2}{(1+2x)^{\frac{1}{2}}} + 2x(1 + 2x)^{\frac{1}{2}}$$

let us now simplify by using $(1 + 2x)^{\frac{1}{2}}$ as the LCM as follows:

$$= \frac{x^2 + 2x\ (1+2x)^{\frac{1}{2}}(1+2x)^{\frac{1}{2}}}{(1+2x)^{\frac{1}{2}}}$$

$$= \frac{x^2 + 2x\ (1+2x)}{(1+2x)^{\frac{1}{2}}} \qquad \text{(Note that } (1 + 2x)^{\frac{1}{2}} \times (1 + 2x)^{\frac{1}{2}} = (1 + 2x)^{\frac{1}{2} + \frac{1}{2}} = 1 + 2x)$$

$$= \frac{x^2 + 2x + 4x^2}{(1+2x)^{\frac{1}{2}}}$$

$$\frac{dy}{dx} = \frac{5x^2 + 2x}{\sqrt{1+2x}}$$

4. Find the derivative of $(2x + 3)^3(4x^2 - 1)^2$

Solution

$$y = (2x + 3)^3(4x^2 - 1)^2$$

Let $u = (2x + 3)^3$

and $v = (4x^2 - 1)^2$

$\dfrac{du}{dx} = 3(2x + 3)^{3-1} \times 2$ (Use of chain rule. Also note that 2 is from the derivative of $2x + 3$)

$\quad = 6(2x + 3)^2$

$\dfrac{dv}{dx} = 2(4x^2 - 1)^{2-1} \times 8x$ (Note that $8x$ is from the derivative of $4x^2 - 1$)

$\quad = 16x(4x^2 - 1)$

Hence, $\dfrac{dy}{dx} = u\dfrac{dv}{dx} + v\dfrac{du}{dx}$

$\quad = (2x + 3)^3 \times 16x(4x^2 - 1) + (4x^2 - 1)^2 \times 6(2x + 3)^2$

Let us factorize the expression by taking out $(2x + 3)^2$ and $(4x^2 - 1)$ which are the common terms as follows:

$\dfrac{dy}{dx} = (2x + 3)^2(4x^2 - 1)[(2x + 3)16x + (4x^2 - 1)6]$

$\quad = (2x + 3)^2(4x^2 - 1)(32x^2 + 48x + 24x^2 - 6)$

$\quad = (2x + 3)^2(4x^2 - 1)(56x^2 + 48x - 6)$

$\quad = (2x + 3)^2(4x^2 - 1)\,2(28x^2 + 24x - 3)$

$\dfrac{dy}{dx} = 2(2x + 3)^2(4x^2 - 1)(28x^2 + 24x - 3)$

5. Differentiate: $y = x(x + 1)(x^2 - 4)$

Solution

$\quad y = x(x + 1)(x^2 - 4)$

Expanding the first two brackets gives:

$\quad y = (x^2 + x)(x^2 - 4)$

Hence, $u = (x^2 + x)$

and $v = (x^2 - 4)$

Hence, $\dfrac{du}{dx} = 2x + 1$

$\dfrac{dv}{dx} = 2x$

Therefore, $\dfrac{dy}{dx} = u\dfrac{dv}{dx} + v\dfrac{du}{dx}$

$\quad = (x^2 + x)2x + (x^2 - 4)(2x + 1)$

$\quad = 2x^3 + 2x^2 + 2x^3 + x^2 - 8x - 4$

$\dfrac{dy}{dx} = 4x^3 + 3x^2 - 8x - 4$

6. Find the derivative of $(x^2 + 3x - 2)^2 \sqrt{x}$

Solution

$\quad y = (x^2 + 3x - 2)^2 \sqrt{x}$

$$u = (x^2 + 3x - 2)^2$$

$$v = \sqrt{x}$$

Or, $v = x^{\frac{1}{2}}$

$\dfrac{du}{dx} = 2(x^2 + 3x - 2)^{2-1} \times 2x + 3$ (Note that $2x + 3$ is from the derivative of $x^2 + 3x - 2$)

$\qquad = (4x + 6)(x^2 + 3x - 2)$

$\dfrac{dv}{dx} = \dfrac{1}{2} x^{-\frac{1}{2}}$ (Note that $8x$ is from the derivative of $4x^2 - 1$)

$\qquad = \dfrac{1}{2x^{\frac{1}{2}}}$

$\dfrac{dv}{dx} = \dfrac{1}{2\sqrt{x}}$

Hence, $\dfrac{dy}{dx} = u\dfrac{dv}{dx} + v\dfrac{du}{dx}$

$\qquad = (x^2 + 3x - 2)^2 \dfrac{1}{2\sqrt{x}} + \sqrt{x}(4x + 6)(x^2 + 3x - 2)$

$\qquad = (x^2 + 3x - 2)^2 \dfrac{1}{2\sqrt{x}} + 2\sqrt{x}(2x + 3)(x^2 + 3x - 2)$

Factorize the expression by taking out ($x^2 + 3x - 2$) which is the common factor. This gives:

$\dfrac{dy}{dx} = (x^2 + 3x - 2)\left[\dfrac{x^2 + 3x - 2}{2\sqrt{x}} + 2\sqrt{x}(2x + 3)\right]$

Simplifying the part in the bracket by taking $2\sqrt{x}$ as the LCM gives:

$\dfrac{dy}{dx} = (x^2 + 3x - 2)\left[\dfrac{x^2 + 3x - 2 + 4x(2x + 3)}{2\sqrt{x}}\right]$ (Note that $2\sqrt{x} \times 2\sqrt{x} = 4x$)

$\qquad = (x^2 + 3x - 2)\left[\dfrac{x^2 + 3x - 2 + 8x^2 + 12x}{2\sqrt{x}}\right]$

$\dfrac{dy}{dx} = \dfrac{(x^2 + 3x - 2)(9x^2 + 15x - 2)}{2\sqrt{x}}$

7. Find the derivative of $(1 + x)(5x - 2)^{\frac{3}{2}}$

<u>Solution</u>

$$y = (1 + x)(5x - 2)^{\frac{3}{2}}$$

$$u = (1 + x)$$

$$v = (5x - 2)^{\frac{3}{2}}$$

$\dfrac{du}{dx} = 1$

$\dfrac{dv}{dx} = \dfrac{3}{2}(5x - 2)^{\frac{3}{2} - 1} \times 5$ (Note that the derivative of $5x - 2$ is 5)

$\qquad = \dfrac{15}{2}(5x - 2)^{\frac{1}{2}}$

Hence, $\dfrac{dy}{dx} = u\dfrac{dv}{dx} + v\dfrac{du}{dx}$

$$= (1 + x) \times \frac{15}{2}(5x - 2)^{\frac{1}{2}} + (5x - 2)^{\frac{3}{2}} \times 1$$

$$= \frac{15}{2}(1 + x)(5x - 2)^{\frac{1}{2}} + (5x - 2)^{\frac{3}{2}}$$

Factorize by taking out $(5x - 2)^{\frac{1}{2}}$ (i.e. the lower exponent) which is the common factor gives:

$$\frac{dy}{dx} = (5x - 2)^{\frac{1}{2}}\left[\frac{15}{2}(1 + x) + 5x - 2\right] \quad \text{(Note that } \frac{(5x-2)^{\frac{3}{2}}}{(5x-2)^{\frac{1}{2}}} = (5x - 2)^{\frac{3}{2}-\frac{1}{2}} = 5x - 2)$$

$$= (5x - 2)^{\frac{1}{2}}\left[\frac{15}{2} + \frac{15x}{2} + 5x - 2\right]$$

$$= (5x - 2)^{\frac{1}{2}}\left[\frac{25x}{2} + \frac{11}{2}\right]$$

$$\frac{dy}{dx} = \sqrt{5x - 2}\left[\frac{25x + 11}{2}\right]$$

8. If y = (1 + x)(2 − 3x)(2x − 1), find $\frac{dy}{dx}$ by using product rule.

<u>Solution</u>

y = (1 + x)(2 − 3x)(2x − 1)

This is a product of three expressions, u, v and w.

Hence, u = (1 + x)

v = (2 − 3x)

and   w = (2x − 1)

Therefore, $\frac{du}{dx} = 1$

$\frac{dv}{dx} = -3$

$\frac{dw}{dx} = 2$

Hence the formula for product rule of three terms is given by:

$$\frac{dy}{dx} = \frac{du}{dx}vw + \frac{dv}{dx}uw + \frac{dw}{dx}uv$$

$$= 1(2 - 3x)(2x - 1) + (-3)(1 + x)(2x - 1) + 2(1 + x)(2 - 3x)$$

$$= 4x - 2 - 6x^2 + 3x + (-3 - 3x)(2x - 1) + (2 + 2x)(2 - 3x)$$

$$= 7x - 2 - 6x^2 - 6x + 3 - 6x^2 + 3x + 4 - 6x + 4x - 6x^2$$

$$= -2 + 3 + 4 + 7x - 6x + 3x - 6x + 4x - 6x^2 - 6x^2 - 6x^2$$

$$\frac{dy}{dx} = 5 + 2x - 18x^2$$

9. Differentiate with respect to x: $(x^2 - 3x + 5)(2x - 7)$

<u>Solution</u>

y = $(x^2 - 3x + 5)(2x - 7)$

Let us differentiate this product by applying product rule but without the use u and v. This is

43

done as follows:

$$\frac{dy}{dx} = (x^2 - 3x + 5)\frac{d(2x-7)}{dx} + (2x-7)\frac{d(x^2-3x+5)}{dx}$$

$$= (x^2 - 3x + 5)2 + (2x - 7)(2x - 3)$$

$$= 2x^2 - 6x + 10 + 4x^2 - 6x - 14x + 21$$

$$\frac{dy}{dx} = 6x^2 - 26x + 31$$

10. If $y = (5x^2 - 3)(2 + \frac{3}{x})$, find $\frac{dy}{dx}$

Solution

$$y = (5x^2 - 3)(2 + \frac{3}{x})$$

$$u = (5x^2 - 3)$$

$$v = (2 + \frac{3}{x})$$

$$\frac{du}{dx} = 10x$$

$$\frac{dv}{dx} = \frac{d(3x^{-1})}{dx} \qquad \text{(Note that } \frac{3}{x} = 3x^{-1})$$

$$= -3x^{-2}$$

$$\frac{dv}{dx} = \frac{-3}{x^2}$$

Hence, $\quad \frac{dy}{dx} = u\frac{dv}{dx} + v\frac{du}{dx}$

$$= (5x^2 - 3)\left(\frac{-3}{x^2}\right) + (2 + \frac{3}{x})10x$$

$$= -15 + \frac{9}{x^2} + 20x + 30$$

$$\frac{dy}{dx} = 15 + 20x + \frac{9}{x^2}$$

Exercise 4

1. If $f(x) = (2x - 1)(3x + 1)$, find $f'(x)$
2. Find the derivative of $y = (3x^2 - 5)(x^2 + 10)$
3. If $y = 5x(3 + x)^{\frac{1}{2}}$ find $\frac{dy}{dx}$
4. Find the derivative of $(x + 5)(x^2 - 7)^3$
5. Differentiate: $y = 2x(3x + 2)(2x^2 - 5)$
6. Find the derivative of $(3x^2 - 1)^3 \sqrt{2x}$

44

7. Find the derivative of $(9 - x)(x + 3)^{\frac{3}{4}}$

8. If $y = (2 - x)(5 - 3x^2)(x + 3)$, find $\dfrac{dy}{dx}$ by using product rule.

9. Differentiate with respect to x: $(3x^4 - x^2 + 2x)(x - 1)$

10. If $y = (3x^2 - x)(1 + \dfrac{1}{2x})$, find $\dfrac{dy}{dx}$

11. Find the derivative of $x^2(\sqrt{x^5})$

12. Find the derivative of $x^4(2x - 11)^{\frac{2}{3}}$

13. If $y = (7 + x)(1 - x^2)(5x^3 + 1)$, find $\dfrac{dy}{dx}$.

14. Differentiate with respect to x: $(3x^4 - x^3 + x^2 + 2x - 3)(5x + 4)$

15. If $y = (x^3 - 3x + 5)\left(\dfrac{1}{x^5}\right)$, find $\dfrac{dy}{dx}$

CHAPTER 5
QUOTIENT RULE OF DERIVATIVE

If y = $\dfrac{u}{v}$ where u and v are functions of x, then:

$$\frac{dy}{dx} = \frac{v\frac{du}{dx} - u\frac{dv}{dx}}{v^2}$$

This is called the quotient rule of differentiation.

Examples

1. If y = $\dfrac{3x^2 - 8x + 5}{5x - 2}$ find $\dfrac{dy}{dx}$

Solution

$$y = \frac{3x^2 - 8x + 5}{5x - 2}$$

This is of the form y = $\dfrac{u}{v}$. Therefore, we are going to apply product rule.

Let   u = $3x^2 - 8x + 5$

and v = $5x - 2$

Hence, $\dfrac{du}{dx}$ = $6x - 8$

$\dfrac{dv}{dx}$ = 5

Therefore, $\dfrac{dy}{dx} = \dfrac{v\frac{du}{dx} - u\frac{dv}{dx}}{v^2}$

$$= \frac{(5x - 2)(6x - 8) - (3x^2 - 8x + 5)(5)}{(5x - 2)^2}$$

$$= \frac{30x^2 - 40x - 12x + 16 - 15x^2 - 40x - 25}{(5x - 2)^2}$$

$$\frac{dy}{dx} = \frac{15x^2 - 12x - 9}{(5x - 2)^2}$$

2. Differentiate with respect to x, the function: $\dfrac{3x^2 - 2x}{x + 5}$

Solution

$$y = \frac{3x^2 - 2x}{x + 5}$$

Let   u = $3x^2 - 2x$

and v = $x + 5$

Hence, $\dfrac{du}{dx}$ = $6x - 2$

$\dfrac{dv}{dx}$ = 1

Therefore, $\dfrac{dy}{dx} = \dfrac{v\frac{du}{dx} - u\frac{dv}{dx}}{v^2}$

$= \dfrac{(x+5)(6x-2) - (3x^2-2x)(1)}{(x+5)^2}$

$= \dfrac{6x^2-2x+30x-10-3x^2+2x}{(x+5)^2}$

$\dfrac{dy}{dx} = \dfrac{3x^2+30x-10}{(x+5)^2}$

3. Find the differential coefficient of $y = \dfrac{-3}{x^2+5}$

Solution

$y = \dfrac{-3}{x^2+5}$

$u = -3$

and $v = x^2+5$

Hence, $\dfrac{du}{dx} = 0$ (The derivative of a constant is zero)

$\dfrac{dv}{dx} = 2x$

Therefore, $\dfrac{dy}{dx} = \dfrac{v\frac{du}{dx} - u\frac{dv}{dx}}{v^2}$

$= \dfrac{(x^2+5) \times 0 - (-3)2x}{(x^2+5)^2}$

$= \dfrac{0-6x}{(x^2+5)^2}$

$\dfrac{dy}{dx} = \dfrac{-6x}{(x^2+5)^2}$

4. Differentiate: $y = \dfrac{\sqrt{3-x}}{\sqrt{3+x}}$

Solution

$y = \dfrac{\sqrt{3-x}}{\sqrt{3+x}}$

$u = \sqrt{3-x}$

$= (3-x)^{\frac{1}{2}}$

and $v = \sqrt{3+x}$

$= (3+x)^{\frac{1}{2}}$

Hence, $\dfrac{du}{dx} = \dfrac{1}{2}(3-x)^{\frac{1}{2}-1} \times -1$ (Note that the derivative of $3-x$ is -1)

$= -\dfrac{1}{2}(3-x)^{-\frac{1}{2}}$

$$\frac{du}{dx} = \frac{-(3-x)^{-\frac{1}{2}}}{2}$$

$$\frac{dv}{dx} = \frac{1}{2}(3+x)^{\frac{1}{2}-1} \text{ x } 1 \quad \text{(Note that the derivative of } 3-x \text{ is } -1)$$

$$= \frac{1}{2}(3+x)^{-\frac{1}{2}}$$

$$\frac{dv}{dx} = \frac{(3+x)^{-\frac{1}{2}}}{2}$$

Therefore, $\dfrac{dy}{dx} = \dfrac{v\frac{du}{dx} - u\frac{dv}{dx}}{v^2}$

$$= \frac{(3+x)^{\frac{1}{2}}\left(\frac{-(3-x)^{-\frac{1}{2}}}{2}\right) - (3-x)^{\frac{1}{2}}\left(\frac{(3+x)^{-\frac{1}{2}}}{2}\right)}{((3+x)^{\frac{1}{2}})^2}$$

Taking out the common terms which are terms with positive exponent in order to factorize the expression gives:

$$\frac{dy}{dx} = \frac{\left((3+x)^{\frac{1}{2}}\right)\left((3-x)^{\frac{1}{2}}\right)\left[\frac{-(3-x)^{-1}}{2} - \frac{(3+x)^{-1}}{2}\right]}{3+x}$$

Note that in order to obtain the terms in the square bracket, we subtracted the exponents of

the factors from the exponents of the original term. For example, $(3+x)^{\frac{1}{2}}\left(\dfrac{-(3-x)^{-\frac{1}{2}}}{2}\right)$ divided

by $\left((3+x)^{\frac{1}{2}}\right)\left((3-x)^{\frac{1}{2}}\right)$ gave $\dfrac{-(3-x)^{-1}}{2}$ since the equal terms canceled out and $-\dfrac{1}{2}-\dfrac{1}{2}=-1$,

which gave the exponent of -1. Similarly, $(3-x)^{\frac{1}{2}}\left(\dfrac{(3+x)^{-\frac{1}{2}}}{2}\right)$ divided by

$\left((3+x)^{\frac{1}{2}}\right)\left((3-x)^{\frac{1}{2}}\right)$ gave $\dfrac{(3+x)^{-1}}{2}$ since the equal terms canceled out and $-\dfrac{1}{2}-\dfrac{1}{2}=-1$, which

gave the exponent of -1 as the terms in the square bracket.

Let us now continue with the solution by simplifying further as follows:

$$\frac{dy}{dx} = \frac{\left((3+x)^{\frac{1}{2}}\right)\left((3-x)^{\frac{1}{2}}\right)\left[\frac{-(3-x)^{-1}}{2} - \frac{(3+x)^{-1}}{2}\right]}{3+x}$$

$$= \frac{\left((3+x)^{\frac{1}{2}}\right)\left((3-x)^{\frac{1}{2}}\right)\left[\frac{-1}{2(3-x)} - \frac{1}{2(3+x)}\right]}{3+x}$$

$$= \frac{\left((3+x)^{\frac{1}{2}}\right)\left((3-x)^{\frac{1}{2}}\right)\left[\frac{-(3+x) - (3-x)}{2(3-x)(3+x)}\right]}{3+x}$$

48

$$= \frac{\left((3+x)^{\frac{1}{2}}\right)\left((3-x)^{\frac{1}{2}}\right)\left[\frac{-3-x-3+x}{2(3-x)(3+x)}\right]}{3+x}$$

$$= \frac{\left((3+x)^{\frac{1}{2}}\right)\left((3-x)^{\frac{1}{2}}\right)\left[\frac{-6}{2(3-x)(3+x)}\right]}{3+x}$$

$$= \frac{\left((3+x)^{\frac{1}{2}}\right)\left((3-x)^{\frac{1}{2}}\right)\left[\frac{-3}{(3-x)(3+x)}\right]}{3+x}$$

$$= \frac{-3\left((3+x)^{\frac{1}{2}}\right)\left((3-x)^{\frac{1}{2}}\right)}{(3-x)(3+x)(3+x)}$$

$$= \frac{-3\left((3+x)^{\frac{1}{2}}\right)\left((3-x)^{\frac{1}{2}}\right)}{(3+x)^2(3-x)}$$

$$= -3(3+x)^{\frac{1}{2}-2}(3-x)^{\frac{1}{2}-1} \quad \text{(Subtraction of exponents due to the division above)}$$

$$= -3(3+x)^{-\frac{3}{2}}(3-x)^{-\frac{1}{2}}$$

$$= \frac{-3}{(3+x)^{\frac{3}{2}}(3-x)^{\frac{1}{2}}}$$

$$= \frac{-3}{\sqrt{(3+x)^3(3-x)}}$$

5. Differentiate with respect to x: $y = \frac{(2x^2-3)^3}{x}$

Solution

$$y = \frac{(2x^2-3)^3}{x}$$
$$u = (2x^2-3)^3$$

and $v = x$

Hence, $\dfrac{du}{dx} = 3(2x^2-3)^{3-1} \times 4x$

$$= 12x(2x^2-3)^2$$

$$\frac{dv}{dx} = 1$$

Therefore, $\dfrac{dy}{dx} = \dfrac{v\dfrac{du}{dx} - u\dfrac{dv}{dx}}{v^2}$

$$= \frac{x[12x(2x^2-3)^2] - (2x^2-3)^3 \times 1}{x^2}$$

$$= \frac{12x^2(2x^2-3)^2 - (2x^2-3)^3}{x^2}$$

Factorize the expression by taking out $(2x^2-3)^2$ which has the lower exponent. This gives:

$$\frac{dy}{dx} = \frac{(2x^2 - 3)^2 [12x^2 - (2x^2 - 3)]}{x^2}$$

$$= \frac{(2x^2 - 3)^2 (12x^2 - 2x^2 + 3)}{x^2}$$

$$\frac{dy}{dx} = \frac{(2x^2 - 3)^2 (10x^2 + 3)}{x^2}$$

6. Find the derivative of $\dfrac{\sqrt{(1 + 2x^2)^3}}{x}$

Solution

$$y = \frac{\sqrt{(1 + 2x^2)^3}}{x}$$

$$u = \sqrt{(1 + 2x^2)^3}$$

$$= [(1 + 2x^2)^3]^{\frac{1}{2}} \quad \text{(When the square root sign is removed, we use an exponent of } \tfrac{1}{2})$$

$$u = (1 + 2x^2)^{\frac{3}{2}} \quad \text{(After multiplying the exponents)}$$

$$v = x$$

Hence, $\dfrac{du}{dx} = \dfrac{3}{2}(1 + 2x^2)^{\frac{3}{2} - 1} \times 4x$ (Note that the derivative of $3 - x$ is -1)

$$= 6x(1 + 2x^2)^{\frac{1}{2}}$$

$$\frac{dv}{dx} = 1$$

Therefore, $\dfrac{dy}{dx} = \dfrac{v\frac{du}{dx} - u\frac{dv}{dx}}{v^2}$

$$= \frac{x\left(6x(1+2x^2)^{\frac{1}{2}}\right) - (1+2x^2)^{\frac{3}{2}} \times 1}{x^2}$$

Take out $(1 + 2x^2)^{\frac{1}{2}}$ which has the lower exponent and factorize the expression. This gives:

$$\frac{dy}{dx} = \frac{(1+2x^2)^{\frac{1}{2}} [6x^2 - (1+2x^2)]}{x^2} \quad \text{(Note that } \frac{(1+2x^2)^{\frac{3}{2}}}{(1+2x^2)^{\frac{1}{2}}} \text{ gives } (1 + 2x^2) \text{ by subtracting exponents.}$$

$$= \frac{(1+2x^2)^{\frac{1}{2}} (6x^2 - 1 - 2x^2)}{x^2}$$

$$= \frac{(1+2x^2)^{\frac{1}{2}} (4x^2 - 1)}{x^2}$$

$$\frac{dy}{dx} = \frac{(\sqrt{1+2x^2})(4x^2 - 1)}{x^2}$$

7. If $y = \dfrac{(4x^3 - 3x^2 + x + 1)^{\frac{1}{2}}}{(x+1)^2}$

Solution

$$y = \dfrac{(4x^3 - 3x^2 + x + 1)^{\frac{1}{2}}}{(x+1)^2}$$

$u = (4x^3 - 3x^2 + x + 1)^{\frac{1}{2}}$ (After multiplying the exponents)

$v = (x + 1)^2$

Hence, $\dfrac{du}{dx} = \dfrac{1}{2}(4x^3 - 3x^2 + x + 1)^{\frac{1}{2} - 1} \times (12x^2 - 6x + 1)$

$$= \dfrac{(12x^2 - 6x + 1)(4x^3 - 3x^2 + x + 1)^{-\frac{1}{2}}}{2}$$

$\dfrac{dv}{dx} = 2(x + 1)^{2-1}$

$= 2(x + 1)$

Therefore, $\dfrac{dy}{dx} = \dfrac{v\dfrac{du}{dx} - u\dfrac{dv}{dx}}{v^2}$

$$= \dfrac{(x+1)^2(12x^2 - 6x + 1)(4x^3 - 3x^2 + x + 1)^{-\frac{1}{2}} - (4x^3 - 3x^2 + x + 1)^{\frac{1}{2}}[2(x+1)]}{2}}{[(x+1)^2]^2}$$

Take out the common terms with lower exponents [i.e. $(x + 1)$ and $(4x^3 - 3x^2 + x + 1)^{-\frac{1}{2}}$] and factorize the expression. This gives:

$$\dfrac{dy}{dx} = \dfrac{\dfrac{(x+1)(4x^3 - 3x^2 + x + 1)^{-\frac{1}{2}}[(x+1)(12x^2 - 6x + 1) - (4x^3 - 3x^2 + x + 1)2]}{2}}{[(x+1)^2]^2}$$

Remember to subtract the exponents of the factors from the exponents of the original expression when simplifying. Simplifying further, the expression above gives:

$$\dfrac{dy}{dx} = \dfrac{(x+1)(4x^3 - 3x^2 + x + 1)^{-\frac{1}{2}}[12x^3 - 6x^2 + x + 12x^2 - 6x + 1 - (8x^3 - 6x^2 + 2x + 2)]}{2(x+1)^4}$$

$$= \dfrac{(x+1)(4x^3 - 3x^2 + x + 1)^{-\frac{1}{2}}(12x^3 - 6x^2 + x + 12x^2 - 6x + 1 - 8x^3 + 6x^2 - 2x - 2)}{2(x+1)^4}$$

$$= \dfrac{(x+1)(4x^3 - 3x^2 + x + 1)^{-\frac{1}{2}}(4x^3 + 12x^2 - 7x - 1)}{2(x+1)^4}$$

$$= \dfrac{(4x^3 - 3x^2 + x + 1)^{-\frac{1}{2}}(4x^3 + 12x^2 - 7x - 1)}{2(x+1)^3}$$

51

Note that $(x + 1)$ cancels out from the numerator and denominator.

Therefore, $\dfrac{dy}{dx} = \dfrac{4x^3 + 12x^2 - 7x - 1}{2(4x^3 - 3x^2 + x + 1)^{\frac{1}{2}}(x+1)^3}$

8. Determine $\dfrac{d}{dx}\left(\dfrac{3 + 2x - x^2}{\sqrt{1+x}}\right)$

Solution

Let $y = \dfrac{3 + 2x - x^2}{\sqrt{1+x}}$

Hence, $u = 3 + 2x - x^2$

$\dfrac{du}{dx} = 2 - 2x$

$v = \sqrt{1 + x}$

$= (1 + x)^{\frac{1}{2}}$

$\dfrac{du}{dx} = \dfrac{1}{2}(1 + x)^{\frac{1}{2} - 1} \times 1$

$= \dfrac{1}{2}(1 + x)^{-\frac{1}{2}}$

Therefore, $\dfrac{dy}{dx} = \dfrac{v\frac{du}{dx} - u\frac{dv}{dx}}{v^2}$

$= \dfrac{(1 + x)^{\frac{1}{2}}(2 - 2x) - (3 + 2x - x^2)\frac{1}{2}(1 + x)^{-\frac{1}{2}}}{[(1 + x)^{\frac{1}{2}}]^2}$

Take out $(1 + x)^{-\frac{1}{2}}$ as the common factor since it has the lower exponent and factorize the expression. This gives:

$\dfrac{dy}{dx} = \dfrac{(1 + x)^{-\frac{1}{2}}\left[(1+x)(2 - 2x) - (3 + 2x - x^2)\frac{1}{2}\right]}{1+x}$

$= \dfrac{(1 + x)^{-\frac{1}{2}}\left[\dfrac{2(1+x)(2 - 2x) - (3 + 2x - x^2)}{2}\right]}{1+x}$

$= \dfrac{(1 + x)^{-\frac{1}{2}}[(2 + 2x)(2 - 2x) - 3 - 2x + x^2]}{2(1+x)}$

$= \dfrac{(1 + x)^{-\frac{1}{2}}(4 - 4x + 4x - 4x^2 - 3 - 2x + x^2)}{2(1+x)}$

$$= \frac{1-2x-3x^2}{2(1+x)^{\frac{1}{2}}(1+x)}$$ 　[When $(1+x)^{-\frac{1}{2}}$ is taken to the denominator it becomes $(1+x)^{\frac{1}{2}}$]

$$\frac{dy}{dx} = \frac{1-2x-3x^2}{2(1+x)^{\frac{3}{2}}}$$ 　(The exponents of same terms have been added together, i.e. $\frac{1}{2}+1=\frac{3}{2}$)

Exercise 5

1. If $y = \dfrac{x^2-5x+1}{x-1}$ find $\dfrac{dy}{dx}$

2. Differentiate with respect to x, the function: $\dfrac{4x^2-x}{2x+3}$

3. Find the differential coefficient of $y = \dfrac{-7}{3x^2+1}$

4. Differentiate: $y = \dfrac{\sqrt{1+x}}{\sqrt{1-x}}$

5. Differentiate with respect to x: $y = \dfrac{(x^3-2)^2}{x^2}$

6. Find the derivative of $\dfrac{\sqrt{2+3x^2}}{x^3}$

7. If $y = \dfrac{(x^2-x-4)^{\frac{1}{3}}}{(2x+1)^2}$

8. Determine $\dfrac{d}{dx}\left(\dfrac{x-2x^3}{\sqrt{2-x}}\right)$

9. Find the differential coefficient of $y = -\dfrac{1}{1-3x^2}$

10. Differentiate: $y = \dfrac{2+x}{2-x}$

CHAPTER 6
DERIVATIVE OF PARAMETRIC EQUATIONS

If y = f(t) and x = g(t) are two different functions of a common variable, t, then the two equations are called parametric equations. The variable t, is the parameter.

The derivative of a parametric equation such as the one stated above is obtained as follows:

$$\frac{dy}{dx} = \frac{\frac{dy}{dt}}{\frac{dx}{dt}}$$

Examples

1. If y = 5 + t^2 and x = 3 − 2t^2, find $\frac{dy}{dx}$

<u>Solution</u>

$$y = 5 + t^2$$

Hence, $\frac{dy}{dt} = 2t$

$$x = 3 - 2t^2$$

Hence, $\frac{dx}{dt} = -4t$

Therefore, $\frac{dy}{dx} = \frac{\frac{dy}{dt}}{\frac{dx}{dt}}$

$$= \frac{2t}{-4t}$$

$$= -\frac{1}{2} \qquad \text{(t cancels out)}$$

2. Find $\frac{dy}{dx}$ of the functions below which are expressed in the parametric form.

$$x = \frac{5}{t^2} \quad \text{and} \quad y = 2t^5 - 3$$

<u>Solution</u>

$$x = \frac{5}{t^2}$$

$$x = 5t^{-2}$$

$$\frac{dx}{dt} = -10t^{-3}$$

$$y = 2t^5 - 3$$

$$\frac{dy}{dt} = 10t^4$$

Therefore, $\frac{dy}{dx} = \frac{\frac{dy}{dt}}{\frac{dx}{dt}}$

$$= \frac{10t^4}{-10t^{-3}}$$

$$= -t^{4-(-3)} \qquad \text{(10 cancels out)}$$

$$= -t^{4+3}$$

$$= -t^7$$

3. If $V = \frac{4}{3}\pi r^3$ and $A = \pi r^2$, find $\frac{dA}{dV}$

<u>Solution</u>

$$V = \frac{4}{3}\pi r^3$$

$$\frac{dV}{dr} = 3\left(\frac{4}{3}\right)\pi r^2$$

$$= 4\pi r^2$$

$$A = \pi r^2$$

$$\frac{dA}{dr} = 2\pi r$$

$$\frac{dA}{dV} = \frac{\frac{dA}{dr}}{\frac{dV}{dr}}$$

$$= \frac{2\pi r}{4\pi r^2}$$

$$\frac{dA}{dV} = \frac{1}{2r}$$

4. Determine the derivative of the curve defined by the equations: $x = t^2 - 4t$ and $y = 2t^3 - 7t$.

<u>Solution</u>

$$y = 2t^3 - 7t$$

Hence, $\frac{dy}{dt} = 6t^2 - 7$

$$x = t^2 - 4t$$

Hence, $\frac{dx}{dt} = 2t - 4$

Therefore, $\frac{dy}{dx} = \frac{\frac{dy}{dt}}{\frac{dx}{dt}}$

$$= \frac{6t^2 - 7}{2t - 4}$$

5. Given that $v = u + at$ and $s = ut + \frac{1}{2}at^2$. Find $\frac{dv}{ds}$ if u and a are constants.

<u>Solution</u>

$$v = u + at$$

$$\frac{dv}{dt} = a$$

$$s = ut + \frac{1}{2}at^2$$

$$\frac{ds}{dt} = u + (2 \times \frac{1}{2} \times at)$$

$$= u + at$$

Hence, $\dfrac{dv}{ds} = \dfrac{\frac{dv}{dt}}{\frac{ds}{dt}}$

$$= \frac{a}{u+at}$$

6. If $y = \dfrac{t}{t-2}$ and $x = \dfrac{1}{t+1}$, find $\dfrac{dy}{dx}$.

Solution

$$y = \frac{t}{t-2}$$

$$\frac{dy}{dt} = \frac{(t-2)(1) - t(1)}{(t-2)^2}$$ (Use of quotient rule where u = t and v = t – 2)

$$= \frac{t-2-t}{(t-2)^2}$$

$$\frac{dy}{dt} = \frac{-2}{(t-2)^2}$$

$$x = \frac{1}{t+1}$$

$$\frac{dx}{dt} = \frac{(t+1)(0) - 1(1)}{(t+1)^2}$$ (Use of quotient rule where u = 1 and v = t + 1)

$$= \frac{-1}{(t+1)^2}$$

Hence, $\dfrac{dy}{dx} = \dfrac{\frac{dy}{dt}}{\frac{dx}{dt}}$

$$= \frac{\frac{-2}{(t-2)^2}}{\frac{-1}{(t+1)^2}}$$

$$= \frac{-2}{(t-2)^2} \times \frac{(t+1)^2}{-1}$$

$$\frac{dy}{dx} = \frac{2(t+1)^2}{(t-2)^2}$$

7. The parametric equations of the motion of a stone are: $y = 12 + 3t - 2t^2$ and $x = 5t$. Find $\dfrac{dy}{dx}$.

Solution

$$y = 12 + 3t - 2t^2$$

$$\frac{dy}{dt} = 3 - 4t$$

$$x = 5t$$

$$\frac{dx}{dt} = 5$$

$$\frac{dy}{dx} = \frac{\frac{dy}{dt}}{\frac{dx}{dt}}$$

$$= \frac{3 - 4t}{5}$$

8. If the parametric equations of a parabola are $y = \frac{2mt^2}{1+t^2}$ and $x = \frac{2m}{1+t^2}$ where m is a constant, find $\frac{dy}{dx}$.

<u>Solution</u>

$$y = \frac{2mt^2}{1+t^2}$$

$$\frac{dy}{dt} = \frac{(1+t^2)(4mt) - 2mt^2(2t)}{(1+t^2)^2} \qquad \text{(Use of quotient rule where u = } 2mt^2 \text{ and v = } 1 + t^2)$$

$$= \frac{4mt + 4mt^3 - 4mt^3}{(1+t^2)^2}$$

$$\frac{dy}{dt} = \frac{4mt}{(1+t^2)^2}$$

$$x = \frac{2m}{1+t^2}$$

$$\frac{dx}{dt} = \frac{(1+t^2)(0) - 2m(2t)}{(1+t^2)^2} \qquad \text{(Use of quotient rule where u = 1 and v = t + 1)}$$

$$= \frac{-4mt}{(1+t^2)^2}$$

Hence, $\frac{dy}{dx} = \frac{\frac{dy}{dt}}{\frac{dx}{dt}}$

$$= \frac{\frac{4mt}{(1+t^2)^2}}{\frac{-4mt}{(1+t^2)^2}}$$

$$= \frac{4mt}{(1+t^2)^2} \times \frac{(1+t^2)^2}{-4mt}$$

$$\frac{dy}{dx} = -1 \qquad \text{(Same terms cancels out)}$$

Exercise 6

1. If $y = t^3 - 5$ and $x = t^2 + 1$ find $\dfrac{dy}{dx}$

2. Find $\dfrac{dy}{dx}$ of the functions below which are expressed in the parametric form:

$$x = \frac{1}{4 - t^3} \text{ and } y = 3 + t^2$$

3. If $V = \dfrac{1}{3}\pi r^2$ and $A = \pi r l + \pi r^2$, find $\dfrac{dV}{dA}$

4. Find the derivative of the curve defined by the equations: $x = 5t^2 - t + 3$ and $y = t^2 - t - 1$.

5. Given that $F = \dfrac{m(v - u)}{t}$ and $s = \dfrac{(u+v)t}{2}$. Find $\dfrac{dF}{ds}$ if u, v and m are constants.

6. If $y = \dfrac{5}{t^2 - 1}$ and $x = \dfrac{3}{t^4 + 1}$, find $\dfrac{dy}{dx}$

7. The parametric equations of the motion of a stone are: $y = t - 3t^4$ and $x = t^2 + 3$. Find $\dfrac{dy}{dx}$.

8. If the parametric equations of a parabola are $y = \dfrac{at^3}{2}$ and $x = \dfrac{at}{5}$ where a is a constant, find $\dfrac{dy}{dx}$.

9. If $V = \dfrac{1}{3}\pi r^3$ and $A = 4\pi r^2$, find $\dfrac{dA}{dV}$

10. Given that $G = 2m + s^2$ and $H = m^2 - \dfrac{3}{s}$. Find $\dfrac{dG}{dH}$ if m is a constant.

CHAPTER 7
DERIVATIVE OF IMPLICIT FUNCTIONS

In the function y = f(x), y is said to be expressed explicitly in terms of x. However, in expressions such as $2xy - x^2y = 5$, the relationship between y and x is said to be implicit.

In order to differentiate implicit functions, y is differentiated just like x but with the addition of $\frac{dy}{dx}$ along with the value obtained.

Examples

1. Differentiate implicitly, the expression: $2x^2 + y^2 = 9$.

<u>Solution</u>

$$2x^2 + y^2 = 9$$

Follow the rule of differentiation and add $\frac{dy}{dx}$ to the value obtained whenever you differentiate y. Hence we differentiate each term in the expression above as follows:

$$\frac{d(2x^2)}{dx} + \frac{d(2y^2)}{dx} = \frac{d(9)}{dx}$$

$$4x + 2y\frac{dy}{dx} = 0 \quad \text{(The derivative of } y^2 \text{ is 2y and the addition of } \frac{dy}{dx} \text{ to 2y gives } 2y\frac{dy}{dx}\text{)}$$

We now make $\frac{dy}{dx}$ the subject of the formula as follows:

$$2y\frac{dy}{dx} = -4x$$

$$\frac{dy}{dx} = \frac{-4x}{2y} \quad \text{(When both sides are divided by 2y)}$$

$$\frac{dy}{dx} = \frac{-2x}{y}$$

2. If $x^3 + y^3 = 18xy$, find $\frac{dy}{dx}$

<u>Solution</u>

$$x^3 + y^3 = 18xy$$

$$3x^2 + 3y^2\frac{dy}{dx} = (18x \times 1\frac{dy}{dx}) + (y \times 18)$$

Note that $18xy$ is differentiated by using product rule where $18x$ is taken as u while y is take as v. Also, the derivative of y is what gave us $1\frac{dy}{dx}$. The above differentiation now simplifies to:

$$3x^2 + 3y^2\frac{dy}{dx} = 18x\frac{dy}{dx} + 18y$$

Collect terms in $\frac{dy}{dx}$ on one side in order to make $\frac{dy}{dx}$ the subject of the formula as follows:

$$3y^2\frac{dy}{dx} - 18x\frac{dy}{dx} = 18y - 3x^2$$

Factorizing the left hand side gives:

$$\frac{dy}{dx}(3y^2 - 18x) = 18y - 3x^2$$

Divide both sides by $3y^2 - 18x$. This gives:

$$\frac{dy}{dx} = \frac{18y - 3x^2}{3y^2 - 18x}$$

$$= \frac{3(6y - x^2)}{3(y^2 - 6x)}$$

$$\frac{dy}{dx} = \frac{6y - x^2}{y^2 - 6x} \qquad \text{(3 cancels out)}$$

3. Find $\frac{dy}{dx}$ given that $x^2y^2 - 3xy + 4xy^3 = 4$

<u>Solution</u>

$$x^2y^2 - 3xy + 4xy^3 = 4$$

Apply product rule to x^2y^2, $3xy$ and $4xy^3$ and differentiate appropriately as follows:

$$(x^2 \times 2y\frac{dy}{dx}) + (y^2 \times 2x) - [(3x \times 1\frac{dy}{dx}) + (y \times 3)] + (4x \times 3y^2\frac{dy}{dx}) + (y^3 \times 4) = 0$$

$$2x^2y\frac{dy}{dx} + 2xy^2 - (3x\frac{dy}{dx} + 3y) + 12xy^2\frac{dy}{dx} + 4y^3 = 0$$

$$2x^2y\frac{dy}{dx} + 2xy^2 - 3x\frac{dy}{dx} - 3y + 12xy^2\frac{dy}{dx} + 4y^3 = 0$$

$$2x^2y\frac{dy}{dx} - 3x\frac{dy}{dx} + 12xy^2\frac{dy}{dx} + 2xy^2 - 3y + 4y^3 = 0$$

$$2x^2y\frac{dy}{dx} - 3x\frac{dy}{dx} + 12xy^2\frac{dy}{dx} = 3y - 2xy^2 - 4y^3$$

Factorizing the left hand side gives:

$$\frac{dy}{dx}(2x^2y - 3x + 12xy^2) = 3y - 2xy^2 - 4y^3$$

$$\frac{dy}{dx} = \frac{3y - 2xy^2 - 4y^3}{2x^2y - 3x + 12xy^2}$$

4. Differentiate $x^4 + 6x^2y^2 - 5 = 0$ implicitly with respect to x.

<u>Solution</u>

$$x^4 + 6x^2y^2 - 5 = 0$$

We differentiate accordingly and apply product rule to $6x^2y^2$ as follows:

$$4x^3 + (6x^2 \times 2y\frac{dy}{dx}) + (y^2 \times 12x) - 0 = 0$$

$$4x^3 + 12x^2y\frac{dy}{dx} + 12xy^2 = 0$$

$$12x^2y\frac{dy}{dx} = -4x^3 - 12xy^2$$

$$\frac{dy}{dx} = \frac{-4x^3 - 12xy^2}{12x^2y}$$

$$= \frac{-4x(x^2 + 3y^2)}{12x^2y}$$

$$\frac{dy}{dx} = \frac{-(x^2 + 3y^2)}{3xy} \qquad \text{(4 and } x \text{ cancels out)}$$

5. Find $\dfrac{dy}{dx}$ if $\dfrac{x^2}{16} + \dfrac{y^2}{25} = 1$

Solution

$$\frac{x^2}{16} + \frac{y^2}{25} = 1$$

$$\frac{2x}{16} + \frac{2y}{25}\frac{dy}{dx} = 0$$

$$\frac{2y}{25}\frac{dy}{dx} = -\frac{2x}{16}$$

$$\frac{2y}{25}\frac{dy}{dx} = -\frac{x}{8}$$

$$\frac{dy}{dx} = \frac{-\dfrac{x}{8}}{\dfrac{2y}{25}}$$

$$= -\frac{x}{8} \times \frac{25}{2y}$$

$$\frac{dy}{dx} = -\frac{25x}{16y}$$

Exercise 7

1. Differentiate implicitly, the expression: $5x^3 + 3y = y^2$.

2. If $2x^2 + 3y^3 = 10$, find $\dfrac{dy}{dx}$

3. Find $\dfrac{dy}{dx}$ given that $xy - 3xy^2 + 4x^3 = 4$

4. Differentiate $2x^2 + xy^2 - 5 = x^3$ implicitly with respect to x.

5. Find $\dfrac{dy}{dx}$ if $\dfrac{x^3}{3} - \dfrac{y^2}{2} = 0$

6. Differentiate implicitly, the expression: $2x^2y + 5y = 1$.

7. If $2x^2y + 4y^3 = 2y$, find $\dfrac{dy}{dx}$

8. Find $\dfrac{dy}{dx}$ given that $5y^2 - 4xy = y$

61

9. Differentiate $x + y^2 - x^2y^2 = 7$ implicitly with respect to x.

10. Find $\dfrac{dy}{dx}$ if $x^5 - \dfrac{3}{y} = 2$

CHAPTER 8
DERIVATIVE OF TRIGONOMETRIC FUNCTIONS

The derivatives of trigonometric functions are as given below:

If y = sin$x$, then $\frac{dy}{dx}$ = cos$x$

If y = cos$x$, then $\frac{dy}{dx}$ = $-$ sin$x$

If y = tan$x$, then $\frac{dy}{dx}$ = sec^2x

If y = cot$x$, then $\frac{dy}{dx}$ = $-$ cosec^2x

If y = sec$x$, then $\frac{dy}{dx}$ = sec$x$tan$x$

If y = cosec$x$, then $\frac{dy}{dx}$ = $-$ cot$x$cosec$x$

Example

1. Find the derivative of cos5x

<u>Solution</u>

    Let y = cos5x

We have to use chain rule from composite function due to 5x which is a function of x.

Hence, let u = 5x

Therefore, y = cosu   (By replacing 5x with u)

    $\frac{du}{dx}$ = 5

    $\frac{dy}{du}$ = $-$ sinu   (Recall that the derivative of cos$x$ is $-$sin$x$)

Therefore, $\frac{dy}{dx}$ = $\frac{dy}{du}$ x $\frac{du}{dx}$ (Chain rule)

    = $-$ sinu x 5

    = $-$ 5sinu

    $\frac{dy}{dx}$ = $-$ 5sin5x (Since u = 5x)

2. If y = sin$\frac{1}{2}$$x$, find $\frac{dy}{dx}$

<u>Solution</u>

    y = sin$\frac{1}{2}$$x$

Let u = $\frac{1}{2}$$x$

Therefore, y = sinu   (By replacing $\frac{1}{2}$$x$ with u)

$$\frac{du}{dx} = \frac{1}{2}$$

$$\frac{dy}{du} = \cos u \quad \text{(Recall that the derivative of } \sin x \text{ is } \cos x\text{)}$$

Therefore, $\dfrac{dy}{dx} = \dfrac{dy}{du} \times \dfrac{du}{dx}$ (Chain rule)

$$= \cos u \times \frac{1}{2}$$

$$= \frac{1}{2}\cos u$$

$$\frac{dy}{dx} = \frac{1}{2}\cos\frac{1}{2}x \quad \text{(Since } u = \frac{1}{2}x\text{)}$$

3. Find the derivative of $5\cos 3x$

<u>Solution</u>

$$y = 5\cos 3x$$

Let $u = 3x$

Therefore, $y = 5\cos u$

$$\frac{du}{dx} = 3$$

$$\frac{dy}{du} = 5(-\sin u) \quad \text{(Note that the constant term i.e. 5 should be used to multiply the derivative)}$$

$$= -5\sin u$$

Therefore, $\dfrac{dy}{dx} = \dfrac{dy}{du} \times \dfrac{du}{dx}$

$$= -5\sin u \times 3$$

$$= -15\sin u$$

$$\frac{dy}{dx} = -15\sin 3x \quad \text{(Since } u = 3x\text{)}$$

4. Find the derivative of $\sin^2 x$

<u>Solution</u>

$$y = \sin^2 x$$

Note that $\sin^2 x = \sin x \times \sin x$

Hence, let $u = \sin x$

Therefore, $y = u^2$ (i.e. u x u from $\sin x \times \sin x$)

$$\frac{du}{dx} = \cos x$$

$$\frac{dy}{du} = 2u$$

Therefore, $\dfrac{dy}{dx} = \dfrac{dy}{du} \times \dfrac{du}{dx}$

$$= 2u \times \cos x$$

$$= 2u\cos x$$

$$\frac{dy}{dx} = 2\sin x\cos x \qquad \text{(Since } u = \sin x\text{)}$$

5. Differentiate with respect to x: $y = \tan 2x$

<u>Solution</u>

$$y = \tan 2x$$

$$\frac{dy}{dx} = \sec^2 2x \times \frac{d(2x)}{dx} \qquad \text{(Note that the derivative of } \tan x \text{ is } \sec^2 x\text{)}$$

$$= \sec^2 2x \times 2$$

$$= 2\sec^2 2x$$

6. If $y = \cos^3 6x^2$, differentiate y with respect to x.

<u>Solution</u>

$$y = \cos^3 6x^2$$

Let us solve this problem without the use of v as follows:

Let $u = \cos 6x^2$

Hence, $y = u^3$

$$\frac{du}{dx} = 12x(-\sin 6x^2) \qquad \text{(Note that } 12x \text{ is from the derivative of } 6x^2\text{)}$$

$$= -12x\sin 6x^2$$

$$\frac{dy}{du} = 3u^2$$

Therefore, $\dfrac{dy}{dx} = \dfrac{dy}{du} \times \dfrac{du}{dx}$

$$= 3u^2 \times (-12x\sin 6x^2)$$

$$= -36xu^2\sin 6x^2$$

$$= -36x(\cos 6x^2)^2\sin 6x^2 \qquad \text{(u has been replaced with } \cos 6x^2\text{)}$$

$$\frac{dy}{dx} = -36x\cos^2 6x^2\sin 6x^2$$

7. Find the derivative of $y = \sec 3x$

<u>Solution</u>

$$y = \sec 3x$$

$$\frac{dy}{dx} = \sec 3x\tan 3x \times \frac{d(3x)}{dx} \qquad \text{(Note that the derivative of } \sec x \text{ is } \sec x\tan x\text{)}$$

$$= \sec 3x\tan 3x \times 3$$

$$\frac{dy}{dx} = 3\sec 3x\tan 3x$$

8. Find the derivative of $\csc 4x^3$

<u>Solution</u>

$$y = \csc 4x^3$$

$$\frac{dy}{dx} = -\csc 4x^3 \cot 4x^3 \; \times \; \frac{d(4x^3)}{dx} \qquad \text{(Note that the derivative of cosec is } -\text{cosec cot)}$$

$$= -\csc 4x^3 \cot 4x^3 \; \times \; 12x^2$$

$$= -12x^2 \csc 4x^3 \cot 4x^3$$

9. Find the derivative of $\cot^2 2x^4$

<u>Solution</u>

$$y = \cot^2 2x^4$$

This can also be written as: $y = \cot 2x^4 \times \cot 2x^4$

Let $u = 2x^4$ (Take the function of x)

Also, let $v = \cot u$ (Take a function of u without taking the exponent)

Hence, $y = v^2$ (Since $v^2 = (\cot u)^2 = (\cot 2x^4)^2 = \cot^2 2x^4$. Hence, $y = v^2$)

$$\frac{du}{dx} = 8x^3$$

$$\frac{dv}{du} = -\csc^2 u$$

$$\frac{dy}{dv} = 2v$$

Therefore, $\dfrac{dy}{dx} = \dfrac{dy}{dv} \; \times \; \dfrac{dv}{du} \; \times \; \dfrac{du}{dx}$

$$= 2v \; \times \; -\csc^2 u \; \times \; 8x^3$$

$$= -16x^3 \, v \csc^2 u$$

$$= -16x^3 \cot u \csc^2 u \qquad \text{(Since } v = \cot u)$$

Substituting in the original value of u gives:

$$\frac{dy}{dx} = -16x^3 \cot 2x^4 \csc^2 2x^4$$

10. Find the derivative of $5x\sin 2x$

<u>Solution</u>

$$y = 5x\sin 2x$$

We are going to apply the product rule of differentiation.

Let $u = 5x$

and $v = \sin 2x$

$$\frac{du}{dx} = 5$$

$$\frac{dv}{dx} = 2\cos 2x \qquad \text{(Note that the differentiation of } 2x \text{ gives 2)}$$

Hence, $\dfrac{dy}{dx} = u\dfrac{dv}{dx} \; + \; v\dfrac{du}{dx}$

$$= (5x \times 2\cos 2x) + (\sin 2x \times 5)$$

$$= 10x\cos 2x \; + \; 5\sin 2x$$

$$\frac{dy}{dx} = 5(2x\cos 2x + \sin 2x)$$

11. Find $\frac{dy}{dx}$ if $y = \frac{1}{x}\sec x$

Solution

$$y = \frac{1}{x}\sec x$$

We apply product rule as follows:

$$u = \frac{1}{x}$$
$$= x^{-1}$$

$$v = \sec 3x$$

$$\frac{du}{dx} = -1x^{-2}$$
$$= \frac{-1}{x^2}$$

$$\frac{dv}{dx} = \sec 3x \tan 3x \times 3$$
$$= 3\sec 3x \tan 3x$$

Note that the derivative of $\sec x$ is $\sec x \tan x$ and 3 is from the derivative of $3x$

Hence, $\frac{dy}{dx} = u\frac{dv}{dx} + v\frac{du}{dx}$

$$= \frac{1}{x}(3\sec 3x \tan 3x) + \sec 3x\left(\frac{-1}{x^2}\right)$$

$$\frac{dy}{dx} = \frac{3}{x}\sec 3x \tan 3x - \frac{1}{x^2}\sec 3x$$

12. Find the derivative of $3\mathrm{cosec}\, x^6$

Solution

$$y = 3\mathrm{cosec}\, x^6$$

Let $u = x^6$

Hence, $y = 3\mathrm{cosec}\, u$

$$\frac{du}{dx} = 6x^5$$

$$\frac{dy}{du} = -3\cot u\, \mathrm{cosec}\, u \quad \text{(The constant term i.e. 5 should be used to multiply the derivative)}$$

Therefore, $\frac{dy}{dx} = \frac{dy}{du} \times \frac{du}{dx}$

$$= -3\cot u\, \mathrm{cosec}\, u \times 6x^5$$

$$= -18x^5 \cot u\, \mathrm{cosec}\, u$$

$$\frac{dy}{dx} = -18x^5 \cot x^6\, \mathrm{cosec}\, x^6 \quad \text{(Since } u = x^6\text{)}$$

13. If $y = \dfrac{1 + \cos 2x}{\sin 2x}$ find $\dfrac{dy}{dx}$.

Solution

$$y = \dfrac{1 + \cos 2x}{\sin 2x}$$

We have to apply quotient rule on this as follows:

$u = 1 + \cos 2x$

$v = \sin 2x$

$\dfrac{du}{dx} = -2\sin 2x$

$\dfrac{dv}{dx} = 2\cos 2x$

Hence, $\dfrac{dy}{dx} = \dfrac{v\dfrac{du}{dx} - u\dfrac{dv}{dx}}{v^2}$ (Quotient rule)

$= \dfrac{\sin 2x(-2\sin 2x) - (1 + \cos 2x)(2\cos 2x)}{(\sin 2x)^2}$

$= \dfrac{-2\sin^2 2x - (2\cos 2x + 2\cos^2 2x)}{\sin^2 2x}$ (Note that $(\sin 2x)^2 = \sin^2 2x$)

$= \dfrac{-2\sin^2 2x - 2\cos 2x - 2\cos^2 2x}{\sin^2 2x}$

$= \dfrac{-2\sin^2 2x - 2\cos^2 2x - 2\cos 2x}{\sin^2 2x}$

$= \dfrac{-2(\sin^2 2x + \cos^2 2x) - 2\cos 2x}{\sin^2 2x}$

$= \dfrac{-2(1) - 2\cos 2x}{\sin^2 2x}$ (Note that $\sin^2 x + \cos^2 x = 1$, hence $\sin^2 2x + \cos^2 2x = 1$)

$\dfrac{dy}{dx} = \dfrac{-2(1 + \cos 2x)}{\sin^2 2x}$

14. Differentiate $y = \dfrac{\sin^2 x}{x}$

Solution

$$y = \dfrac{\sin^2 x}{x}$$

This is also quotient rule.

Therefore, $u = \sin^2 x$

$v = x$

Let us follow a direct and systematic way of differentiating trigonometric functions.

Hence, in order to differentiate $\sin 2x$:

First, differentiate the exponent of $\sin^2$ without changing the trigonometric term. This gives:

$2\sin^{2-1}$

$= 2\sin$

68

Then add the term in x. This gives:

$2\sin x$

The next step is to differentiate sin which gives cos. Also add the term in x to obtain $\cos x$.

Finally, differentiate the term in x. Hence, differentiating x gives 1.

Now multiply the three terms obtained in the three steps above. This gives:

$2\sin x \ \times \ \cos x \ \times \ 1$

$= 2\sin x\cos x$

Hence, $\dfrac{du}{dx} = 2\sin x\cos x$ \qquad (As obtained above)

Since, $v = x$

Then, $\dfrac{dv}{dx} = 1$

Hence, $\dfrac{dy}{dx} = \dfrac{v\dfrac{du}{dx} - u\dfrac{dv}{dx}}{v^2}$

$= \dfrac{x(2\sin x\cos x) - \sin^2 x(1)}{x^2}$

$= \dfrac{2x\sin x\cos x - \sin^2 x}{x^2}$

$= \dfrac{\sin x(2x\cos x - \sin x)}{x^2}$

15. Differentiate with respect to x: $\dfrac{\sec 2x}{x^3 + 1}$

Solution

$y = \dfrac{\sec 2x}{x^3 + 1}$

$u = \sec 2x$

$v = x^3 + 1$

Hence, $\dfrac{du}{dx} = 2\sec 2x\tan 2x$

Then, $\dfrac{dv}{dx} = 3x^2$

Hence, $\dfrac{dy}{dx} = \dfrac{v\dfrac{du}{dx} - u\dfrac{dv}{dx}}{v^2}$

$= \dfrac{(x^3 + 1)(2\sec 2x\tan 2x) - \sec 2x(3x^2)}{(x^3 + 1)^2}$

$= \dfrac{(x^3 + 1)(2\sec 2x\tan 2x) - 3x^2\sec 2x}{(x^3 + 1)^2}$

16. Find the derivative of $\dfrac{\cos \sqrt{x}}{1 + x}$

Solution

$$y = \frac{\cos \sqrt{x}}{1 + x}$$

$$u = \cos\sqrt{x}$$

$$= \cos x^{\frac{1}{2}}$$

$$v = 1 + x$$

Hence, $\dfrac{du}{dx} = \dfrac{d(x^{\frac{1}{2}})}{dx} \times \dfrac{d(\cos)}{dx}$

Note that $\dfrac{d(\cos)}{dx}$ means the derivative of cos which gives $-\sin$, and then $x^{\frac{1}{2}}$ is added to it to give $-\sin x^{\frac{1}{2}}$. Hence we continue as follows:

$$\frac{du}{dx} = \frac{1}{2}x^{-\frac{1}{2}} \times -\sin x^{\frac{1}{2}}$$

$$= \frac{1}{2x^{\frac{1}{2}}} \times -\sin x^{\frac{1}{2}}$$

$$\frac{du}{dx} = \frac{-\sin x^{\frac{1}{2}}}{2x^{\frac{1}{2}}}$$

Also, $\dfrac{dv}{dx} = 1$

Hence, $\dfrac{dy}{dx} = \dfrac{v\frac{du}{dx} - u\frac{dv}{dx}}{v^2}$

$$= \frac{(1+x)\left(\dfrac{-\sin x^{\frac{1}{2}}}{2x^{\frac{1}{2}}}\right) - \cos x^{\frac{1}{2}}(1)}{(1+x)^2}$$

$$= \frac{-\sin \sqrt{x}}{2\sqrt{x}(1+x)} - \frac{\cos \sqrt{x}}{(1+x)^2} \qquad \text{(When the fractions are separated)}$$

$$\frac{dy}{dx} = \frac{-(1+x)\sin \sqrt{x} - 2\sqrt{x}\cos \sqrt{x}}{2\sqrt{x}(1+x)^2} \qquad \text{(When the fractions are combined)}$$

17. Find $\dfrac{dy}{dx}$ if $y = \dfrac{1-x^2}{1+\cos x}$

<u>Solution</u>

$$y = \frac{1-x^2}{1+\cos x}$$

$$u = 1 - x^2$$

$$v = 1 + \cos x$$

$$\frac{du}{dx} = -2x$$

$$\frac{dv}{dx} = -\sin x$$

70

Hence, $\dfrac{dy}{dx} = \dfrac{v\frac{du}{dx} - u\frac{dv}{dx}}{v^2}$

$= \dfrac{(1+\cos x)(-2x) - (1-x^2)(-\sin x)}{(1 + \cos x)^2}$

$\dfrac{dy}{dx} = \dfrac{-2x(1+\cos x) + (1-x^2)\sin x}{(1 + \cos x)^2}$

Note that the negative sign from $-\sin x$ changed the negative sign at the middle to a positive sign since negative sign multiplied by negative sign gives a positive sign.

18. Find the derivative of $8x\sin x^2$

Solution

   $y = 8x\sin x^2$

We apply product rule as follows:

   $u = 8x$

   $\dfrac{du}{dx} = 8$

   $v = \sin x^2$

   $\dfrac{dv}{dx} = \dfrac{d(\sin)}{dx} \times \dfrac{d(x^2)}{dx}$

   $= \cos x^2 \times 2x$

   $= 2x\cos x^2$

Note that $\dfrac{d(\sin)}{dx}$ gives cos which result to $\cos x^2$ when x^2 from the question is added

Hence, $\dfrac{dy}{dx} = u\dfrac{dv}{dx} + v\dfrac{du}{dx}$

   $= 8x(2x\cos x^2) + \sin x^2(8)$

   $= 16x^2\cos x^2 + 8\sin x^2$

$\dfrac{dy}{dx} = 8(2x^2\cos x^2 + \sin x^2)$

19. Differentiate with respect to x: $\sec 2x\sin^3 2x$

Solution

   $y = \sec 2x\sin^3 2x$

We apply product rule as follows:

   $u = \sec 2x$

   $\dfrac{du}{dx} = \dfrac{d(\sec)}{dx} \times \dfrac{d(2x)}{dx}$

   $= \sec 2x\tan 2x \times 2$

   $\dfrac{du}{dx} = 2\sec 2x\tan 2x$

Note that $\dfrac{d(\sec)}{dx}$ gives sectan, but remember to add $2x$ after sec and tan respectively to obtain sec2xtan2x

$v = \sin^3 2x$

In order to directly differentiate a trigonometric term with exponent like this (i.e. $\sin^3$) we have three solutions to multiply as follows:

First solution: consider only the exponent and differentiate $\sin^3$. This gives:

$\dfrac{d(\sin^3)}{dx} = 3\sin^2$

We now add $2x$ from the question to obtain $3\sin^2 2x$

Second solution: $\dfrac{d(\sin)}{dx} = \cos$ which gives $\cos 2x$

Third solution: $\dfrac{d(2x)}{dx} = 2$

Multiply theses three solutions to give the derivative of $v = \sin^3 2x$ as follows:

$\dfrac{dv}{dx} = 3\sin^2 2x \times \cos 2x \times 2$

$\qquad = 6\sin^2 2x \cos 2x$

Now, $\dfrac{dy}{dx} = u\dfrac{dv}{dx} + v\dfrac{du}{dx}$

$= \sec 2x(6\sin^2 2x\cos 2x) + \sin^3 2x(2\sec 2x\tan 2x)$

$= \dfrac{1}{\cos 2x}(6\sin^2 2x\cos 2x) + \sin^3 2x(2\dfrac{1}{\cos 2x}\dfrac{\sin 2x}{\cos 2x})$ (Note that $\sec 2x = \dfrac{1}{\cos 2x}$ and $\tan 2x = \dfrac{\sin 2x}{\cos 2x}$)

$= 6\sin^2 2x + 2\sin^2 2x(\dfrac{\sin 2x}{\cos 2x}\dfrac{\sin 2x}{\cos 2x})$

Note that one $\sin 2x$ has been taken out of $\sin^3 2x$ and placed inside the bracket.

$= 6\sin^2 2x + 2\sin^2 2x(\tan 2x\tan x)$ (Since $\dfrac{\sin 2x}{\cos 2x} = \tan 2x$)

$= 6\sin^2 2x + 2\sin^2 2x(\tan^2 2x)$

$\dfrac{dy}{dx} = 2\sin^2 2x(3 + \tan^2 2x)$ (After factorization)

20. Differentiate with respect to x: $\dfrac{\sec x - \tan x}{\sec x + \tan x}$

<u>Solution</u>

$y = \dfrac{\sec x - \tan x}{\sec x + \tan x}$

$u = \sec x - \tan x$

$\dfrac{du}{dx} = \sec x\tan x - \sec^2 x$

$v = \sec x + \tan x$

$\dfrac{dv}{dx} = \sec x\tan x + \sec^2 x$

$$\frac{dy}{dx} = \frac{v\frac{du}{dx} - u\frac{dv}{dx}}{v^2}$$

$$= \frac{(\sec x + \tan x)(\sec x\tan x - \sec 2x) - (\sec x - \tan x)(\sec x\tan x + \sec 2x)}{(\sec x + \tan x)^2}$$

Expanding bracket in the numerator gives:

$$\frac{dy}{dx} = \frac{\sec^2 x\tan x - \sec^3 x + \sec x\tan^2 x - \sec^2 x\tan x - [\sec^2 x\tan x + \sec^3 x - \sec x\tan^2 x - \sec^2 x\tan x]}{(\sec x + \tan x)^2}$$

$$= \frac{\sec^2 x\tan x - \sec^3 x + \sec x\tan^2 x - \sec^2 x\tan x - \sec^2 x\tan x - \sec^3 x + \sec x\tan^2 x + \sec^2 x\tan x]}{(\sec x + \tan x)^2}$$

$$= \frac{2\sec x\tan^2 x - 2\sec^3 x}{(\sec x + \tan x)^2} \qquad \text{(Note that all the sec}^2x\text{tan}x \text{ have cancelled out)}$$

$$= \frac{2\sec x(\tan^2 x - \sec^2 x)}{(\sec x + \tan x)^2}$$

$$= \frac{2\sec x(-1)}{(\sec x + \tan x)^2} \qquad \text{(Note that tan}^2x - \text{sec}^2x = -1)$$

$$= \frac{-2\sec x}{(\sec x + \tan x)^2}$$

$$\frac{dy}{dx} = -\frac{2\sec x}{(\sec x + \tan x)^2}$$

21. Find the derivative of $\sqrt{\dfrac{\cos 2x}{1 + \sin 2x}}$

Solution

$$y = \sqrt{\frac{\cos 2x}{1 + \sin 2x}}$$

This can also be written as:

$$y = \frac{(\cos 2x)^{\frac{1}{2}}}{(1 + \sin 2x)^{\frac{1}{2}}}$$

$$u = (\cos 2x)^{\frac{1}{2}}$$

Using the chain rule, we obtain $\dfrac{du}{dx}$ as follows:

$$\frac{du}{dx} = \frac{1}{2}(\cos 2x)^{\frac{1}{2}-1} \times \frac{d(\cos 2x)}{dx}$$

$$= \frac{1}{2}(\cos 2x)^{-\frac{1}{2}} \times -2\sin 2x$$

$$= \frac{-2\sin 2x}{2(\cos 2x)^{\frac{1}{2}}}$$

$$= \frac{-\sin 2x}{(\cos 2x)^{\frac{1}{2}}}$$

$$v = (1 + \sin 2x)^{\frac{1}{2}}$$

73

$$\frac{dv}{dx} = \frac{1}{2}(1 + \sin 2x)^{\frac{1}{2} - 1} \times \frac{d(1 + \sin 2x)}{dx}$$

$$= \frac{1}{2}(1 + \sin 2x)^{-\frac{1}{2}} \times 2\cos 2x$$

$$= \frac{2\cos 2x}{2(1 + \sin 2x)^{\frac{1}{2}}}$$

$$= \frac{\cos 2x}{(1 + \sin 2x)^{\frac{1}{2}}}$$

$$\frac{dy}{dx} = \frac{v\frac{du}{dx} - u\frac{dv}{dx}}{v^2}$$

$$= \frac{(1 + \sin 2x)^{\frac{1}{2}}\left(\dfrac{-\sin 2x}{(\cos 2x)^{\frac{1}{2}}}\right) - (\cos 2x)^{\frac{1}{2}}\left(\dfrac{\cos 2x}{(1 + \sin 2x)^{\frac{1}{2}}}\right)}{[(1 + \sin 2x)^{\frac{1}{2}}]^2}$$

$$= \frac{\left(\dfrac{-\sin 2x(1 + \sin 2x)^{\frac{1}{2}}}{(\cos 2x)^{\frac{1}{2}}}\right) - \left(\dfrac{\cos 2x(\cos 2x)^{\frac{1}{2}}}{(1 + \sin 2x)^{\frac{1}{2}}}\right)}{1 + \sin 2x}$$

$$= \frac{\left(\dfrac{-\sin 2x(1 + \sin 2x) - \cos 2x(\cos 2x)}{(\cos 2x)^{\frac{1}{2}}(1 + \sin 2x)^{\frac{1}{2}}}\right)}{1 + \sin 2x}$$

Note that $(\cos 2x)^{\frac{1}{2}} \times (\cos 2x)^{\frac{1}{2}} = \cos 2x$ (Since the exponents are added). Similarly:

$(1 + \sin 2x)^{\frac{1}{2}} \times (1 + \sin 2x)^{\frac{1}{2}} = 1 + \sin 2x$. Simplifying the above expression further, gives:

$$\frac{dy}{dx} = \frac{-\sin 2x(1 + \sin 2x) - \cos^2 2x}{(\cos 2x)^{\frac{1}{2}}(1 + \sin 2x)^{\frac{1}{2}}(1 + \sin 2x)}$$

$$= \frac{-\sin 2x - \sin^2 2x - \cos^2 2x}{(\cos 2x)^{\frac{1}{2}}(1 + \sin 2x)^{\frac{1}{2}}(1 + \sin 2x)}$$

$$= \frac{-\sin 2x - (\sin^2 2x + \cos^2 2x)}{(\cos 2x)^{\frac{1}{2}}(1 + \sin 2x)^{\frac{1}{2}}(1 + \sin 2x)}$$

$$= \frac{-\sin 2x - 1}{(\cos 2x)^{\frac{1}{2}}(1 + \sin 2x)^{\frac{1}{2}}(1 + \sin 2x)} \qquad \text{(Note that } \sin^2 2x + \cos^2 2x = 1)$$

$$= \frac{-(1 + \sin 2x)}{(\cos 2x)^{\frac{1}{2}}(1 + \sin 2x)^{\frac{1}{2}}(1 + \sin 2x)}$$

$$= \frac{-1}{(\cos 2x)^{\frac{1}{2}}(1 + \sin 2x)^{\frac{1}{2}}} \qquad \text{(Note that } 1 + \sin 2x \text{ cancels out)}$$

22. Differentiate with respect to x: $\sin x - 2x\cos x$

Solution

$y = \sin x - 2x\cos x$

Treat $2x\cos x$ using product rule.

$$\frac{dy}{dx} = \frac{d(\sin x)}{dx} - \left(2x\,\frac{d(\cos x)}{dx} + \cos x\,\frac{d(2x)}{dx}\right)$$

$$= \cos x - [2x(-\sin x) + \cos x(2)]$$

$$= \cos x + 2x\sin x - 2\cos x$$

$$= 2x\sin x - \cos x$$

23. Find the derivative of $\cos^5 3x^4$

Solution

$y = \cos^5 3x^4$

A direct way of differentiating this problem is applied as follows:

$$\frac{dy}{dx} = \frac{d(\cos^5)}{dx} \times \frac{d(\cos)}{dx} \times \frac{d(3x^4)}{dx}$$

$$= 5\cos^4 3x^4 \times (-\sin 3x^4) \times 12x^3$$

Note that the derivative of $\cos^5$ gives $5\cos^4$ (do not change the trigonometric term, i.e. cos) and then the addition of $3x^4$ from the question gives $5\cos^4 3x^4$.

Similarly the derivative of cos gives $-\sin$ and the addition of $3x^4$ from the question gives $-\sin 3x^4$.

Hence, multiplying the terms above gives:

$$\frac{dy}{dx} = -60x^3\cos^4 3x^4\sin 3x^4$$

24. Differentiate with respect to x: $\sin^8 15x^6$

Solution

$y = \sin^8 15x^6$

We can also differentiate this problem directly as follows:

$$\frac{dy}{dx} = \frac{d(\sin^8)}{dx} \times \frac{d(\sin)}{dx} \times \frac{d(15x^6)}{dx}$$

$$= 8\sin^7 15x^6 \times \cos 15x^6 \times 90x^5$$

Note that the derivative of $\sin^8$ gives $8\sin^7$ (in this case do not change the trigonometric term, i.e. sin) and then the addition of $15x^6$ from the question gives $8\sin^7 15x^6$.

Similarly the derivative of sin gives cos and the addition of $15x^6$ from the question gives $\cos 15x^6$. Hence, we continue as follows:

$$\frac{dy}{dx} = 8\sin^7 15x^6 \times \cos 15x^6 \times 90x^5$$

$$= 720x^5\sin^7 15x^6\cos 15x^6$$

Exercise 8

1. Find the derivative of $\tan 2x$

2. If $y = \cos\dfrac{1}{5}x$, find $\dfrac{dy}{dx}$

3. Find the derivative of $10\cos 5x$

4. Find the derivative of $\sin^3 x$

5. Differentiate with respect to x: $y = \tan^2 x$

6. If $y = \sin^4 3x^5$, differentiate y with respect to x.

7. Find the derivative of $y = \operatorname{cosec} 6x^2$

8. Find the derivative of $\sec 2x^5$

9. Find the derivative of $\tan 3x^2$

10. Find the derivative of $x^2\cos 3x$

11. Find $\dfrac{dy}{dx}$ if $y = \dfrac{3}{x^3}\sin 2x$

12. Find the derivative of $12\sec x^4$

13. If $y = \dfrac{2-\sin 5x}{\tan x}$ find $\dfrac{dy}{dx}$.

14. Differentiate $y = \dfrac{\sin^3 x}{2x}$

15. Differentiate with respect to x: $\dfrac{\cot 2x}{x+3}$

16. Find the derivative of $\dfrac{\sin\sqrt[3]{3}}{5x}$

17. Find $\dfrac{dy}{dx}$ if $y = \dfrac{x^2-3}{\sec 2x}$

18. Find the derivative of $3x^2\cos 3x^2$

19. Differentiate with respect to x: $\cot x\cos^2 x$

20. Differentiate with respect to x: $\dfrac{\sin x - \cos x}{\sin x + \cos x}$

21. Find the derivative of $\dfrac{\sec 4x}{\cos 4x - 2}$

22. Differentiate with respect to x: $\cos 3x - x^2\sec x$

23. Find the derivative of $\sin^9 x^3$

24. Differentiate with respect to x: $\sin 6x^{\frac{1}{2}}$

25. Find $\dfrac{dy}{dx}$ if $y = \dfrac{1}{x^2}\sin x^3$

26. Find the derivative of $\cos^3 2x^5$

27. If $y = \dfrac{\cos 10x}{\sin 2x}$ find $\dfrac{dy}{dx}$.

28. Differentiate $y = \dfrac{3\sin x^4}{2x}$

29. Differentiate with respect to x: $\dfrac{\tan 5x}{2x - 1}$

30. Find the derivative of $\dfrac{\tan^2 x}{2x}$

CHAPTER 9
DERIVATIVE OF INVERSE FUNCTIONS

If the derivative of a function is given by $\dfrac{dy}{dx}$, then the derivative of the inverse function is given

by: $\dfrac{1}{\frac{dy}{dx}} = \dfrac{dx}{dy}$

Or, $\dfrac{dy}{dx} = \dfrac{1}{\frac{dx}{dy}}$

Examples

1. Find $\dfrac{dx}{dy}$ if $y = \sqrt[3]{x}$

<u>Solution</u>

Method 1

$$y = \sqrt[3]{x}$$

Or $y = x^{\frac{1}{3}}$

Let us make x the subject of the formula. The inverse of $\dfrac{1}{3}$ is 3. Hence raise both sides to the

exponent 3 as follows:

$$y^3 = (x^{\frac{1}{3}})^3$$

$$y^3 = x^1 \qquad \text{(Note that 1 was obtained from } \dfrac{1}{3} \times 3\text{)}$$

Hence, $x = y^3$

Therefore, $\dfrac{dx}{dy} = 3y^2$

Method 2

$$y = \sqrt[3]{x}$$

Or $y = x^{\frac{1}{3}}$

$$\dfrac{dy}{dx} = \dfrac{1}{3}x^{\frac{1}{3}-1}$$

$$= \dfrac{1}{3}x^{-\frac{2}{3}}$$

$$\dfrac{dy}{dx} = \dfrac{1}{3x^{\frac{2}{3}}}$$

Hence, $\dfrac{dx}{dy} = \dfrac{1}{\frac{dy}{dx}}$

$$= \dfrac{3x^{\frac{2}{3}}}{1} \qquad \text{(This means the inverse of } \dfrac{1}{3x^{\frac{2}{3}}}\text{)}$$

$= 3x^{\frac{2}{3}}$

$= 3(\sqrt[3]{x})^2$ [Recall from indices that $x^{\frac{a}{b}} = (\sqrt[b]{x})^a$]

$\frac{dx}{dy} = 3y^2$ (Since $y = \sqrt[3]{x}$)

2. If $y = \sqrt[5]{2x - 3}$ find $\frac{dx}{dy}$

Solution

$\quad y = \sqrt[5]{2x - 3}$

Or $y = (2x - 3)^{\frac{1}{5}}$

Let us make x the subject of the formula. The inverse of $\frac{1}{5}$ is 5. Hence raise both sides to the

exponent 5 as follows:

$\quad y^5 = [(2x - 3)^{\frac{1}{5}}]^5$

$\quad y^5 = 2x - 3$ (Note that $\frac{1}{5}$ x 5 = 1, which cancels the fractional exponent)

Hence, $2x = y^5 + 3$

$\quad x = \dfrac{y^5 + 3}{2}$

$\quad x = \dfrac{y^5}{2} + \dfrac{3}{2}$ (When we separate into fractions by dividing each part by the denominator)

Therefore, $\dfrac{dx}{dy} = \dfrac{5y^4}{2}$

3. If $y = x^3 - 5$. Find $\frac{dx}{dy}$

Solution

$\quad y = x^3 - 5$

$\quad y + 5 = x^3$

$\quad x^3 = y + 5$

$\quad x = (y + 5)^{\frac{1}{3}}$ (By raising both sides to an exponent of the inverse of 3 which is $\frac{1}{3}$)

$\quad \dfrac{dx}{dy} = \dfrac{1}{3}(y + 5)^{\frac{1}{3} - 1}$ x 1

Note that the 1 was obtained from the derivative of y + 5 since chain rule was used.

$\quad \dfrac{dx}{dy} = \dfrac{1}{3}(y + 5)^{-\frac{2}{3}}$

$\quad \dfrac{dx}{dy} = \dfrac{1}{3(y+5)^{\frac{2}{3}}}$

Recall from indices that $x^{\frac{a}{b}} = (\sqrt[b]{x})^a$. Applying this rule gives:

$$\frac{dx}{dy} = \frac{1}{3[\sqrt[3]{(y+5)^2}]}$$

4. If $y = \frac{1}{2}x^4 + 3$, find $\frac{dx}{dy}$

Solution

$$y = \frac{1}{2}x^4 + 3$$

$$y - 3 = \frac{1}{2}x^4$$

$$2(y - 3) = x^4$$

$$x^4 = 2y - 6$$

$$x = (2y - 6)^{\frac{1}{4}} \quad \text{(This is obtained by raising both sided to an exponent of the inverse of 4, i.e. } \frac{1}{4})$$

Hence we use chain rule to determine $\frac{dx}{dy}$ as follows:

$$\frac{dx}{dy} = \frac{1}{4}(2y - 6)^{\frac{1}{4} - 1} \times 2 \quad \text{(Note that 2 is from the derivative of } 2y - 6)$$

$$\frac{dx}{dy} = \frac{1}{2}(2y - 6)^{-\frac{3}{4}}$$

$$\frac{dx}{dy} = \frac{1}{2(2y - 6)^{\frac{3}{4}}}$$

Hence, $\frac{dx}{dy} = \frac{1}{2[\sqrt[4]{(2y-6)^3}]} \quad$ [This is obtained from the law of indices given by: $x^{\frac{a}{b}} = (\sqrt[b]{x})^a$]

5. If $y = \frac{x + 2}{x}$, find $\frac{dx}{dy}$.

Solution

$$y = \frac{x + 2}{x}$$

$$xy = x + 2 \quad \text{(When we cross multiply)}$$

$$xy - x = 2$$

Factorizing the left hand side gives:

$$x(y - 1) = 2$$

$$x = \frac{2}{y - 1}$$

$$x = 2(y - 1)^{-1} \quad \text{(Take note of the use of negative exponent when the denominator goes up)}$$

Hence we use chain rule to determine $\frac{dx}{dy}$ as follows:

$$\frac{dx}{dy} = -1 \times 2(y - 1)^{-1-1} \times 1 \quad \text{(Note that 1 is from the derivative of } y - 1)$$

$$\frac{dx}{dy} = -2(y-1)^{-2}$$

$$\frac{dx}{dy} = \frac{-2}{(y-1)^2}$$

6. Find $\frac{dx}{dy}$ if $y = \frac{1}{x+2}$

<u>Solution</u>

$$y = \frac{1}{x+2}$$

$$x + 2 = \frac{1}{y}$$

$$x = \frac{1}{y} - 2$$

$$x = y^{-1} - 2$$

$$\frac{dx}{dy} = -1 \times y^{-1-1}$$

$$= -y^{-2}$$

$$\frac{dx}{dy} = \frac{-1}{y^2}$$

7. Find $\frac{dx}{dy}$ if $y = x^{\frac{2}{3}}$

<u>Solution</u>

$$y = x^{\frac{2}{3}}$$

Raise both sides to the exponent $\frac{3}{2}$ i.e. the inverse of $\frac{2}{3}$. This gives:

$$y^{\frac{3}{2}} = (x^{\frac{2}{3}})^{\frac{3}{2}}$$

$$y^{\frac{3}{2}} = x \quad \text{(Note that } \frac{2}{3} \times \frac{3}{2} = 1, \text{ and } x^1 = x\text{)}$$

$$x = y^{\frac{3}{2}}$$

$$\frac{dx}{dy} = \frac{3}{2} \times y^{\frac{3}{2}-1}$$

$$= \frac{3}{2} y^{\frac{1}{2}}$$

$$\frac{dx}{dy} = \frac{3\sqrt{y}}{2}$$

8. If $y = (5x + 7)^{\frac{3}{10}}$ find $\frac{dx}{dy}$.

<u>Solution</u>

$$y = (5x + 7)^{\frac{3}{10}}$$

Raise both sides to the exponent $\frac{10}{3}$ i.e. the inverse of $\frac{3}{10}$. This gives:

$$y^{\frac{10}{3}} = [(5x + 7)^{\frac{3}{10}}]^{\frac{10}{3}}$$

$$y^{\frac{10}{3}} = 5x + 7 \quad \text{(Note that } \frac{3}{10} \times \frac{10}{3} = 1\text{)}$$

$$y^{\frac{10}{3}} - 7 = 5x$$

$$x = \frac{y^{\frac{10}{3}} - 7}{5}$$

$$= \frac{y^{\frac{10}{3}}}{5} - \frac{7}{5}$$

$$x = \frac{1}{5} y^{\frac{10}{3}} - \frac{7}{5}$$

$$\frac{dx}{dy} = \frac{10}{3} \times \frac{1}{5} y^{\frac{10}{3} - 1}$$

$$= \frac{2}{3} y^{\frac{7}{3}}$$

$$\frac{dx}{dy} = \frac{2\sqrt[3]{y^7}}{3}$$

Exercise 9

1. Find $\dfrac{dx}{dy}$ if $y = 7x^3$

2. If $y = \sqrt[3]{1 + x^2}$ find $\dfrac{dx}{dy}$

3. If $y = 2x^5 - 3$. Find $\dfrac{dx}{dy}$

4. If $y = \dfrac{2}{3}x^3 - 9$, find $\dfrac{dx}{dy}$

5. If $y = \dfrac{2x + 1}{x}$, find $\dfrac{dx}{dy}$.

6. Find $\dfrac{dx}{dy}$ if $y = \dfrac{3}{x^2 - 5}$

7. Find $\dfrac{dx}{dy}$ if $y = 2x^{\frac{1}{4}}$

8. If $y = (x - 3)^{\frac{1}{5}}$ find $\dfrac{dx}{dy}$.

9. If $y = \dfrac{4x + 5}{x}$, find $\dfrac{dx}{dy}$.

10. Find $\dfrac{dx}{dy}$ if $y = \dfrac{1}{x^3 + 8}$

CHAPTER 10
DERIVATIVES OF INVERSE TRIGONOMETRIC FUNCTIONS

Recall that if $\sin x = y$, then $x = \sin^{-1}y$. This is referred to as inverse trigonometric function. The derivatives of inverse trigonometric functions are given below.

If $y = \sin^{-1}x$, then $\dfrac{dy}{dx} = \dfrac{1}{\sqrt{1-x^2}}$

If $y = \cos^{-1}x$, then $\dfrac{dy}{dx} = \dfrac{-1}{\sqrt{1-x^2}}$

If $y = \tan^{-1}x$, then $\dfrac{dy}{dx} = \dfrac{1}{1+x^2}$

If $y = \cot^{-1}x$, then $\dfrac{dy}{dx} = \dfrac{-1}{1+x^2}$

If $y = \sec^{-1}x$, then $\dfrac{dy}{dx} = \dfrac{1}{x\sqrt{x^2-1}}$

If $y = \text{cosec}^{-1}x$, then $\dfrac{dy}{dx} = \dfrac{-1}{x\sqrt{x^2-1}}$

Note that $\sin^{-1}x$ can also be written as $\arcsin x$. Other inverse function can be written in a similar way.

Examples

1. If $y = \cos^{-1}x$ find the $\dfrac{dy}{dx}$.

Solution

$$y = \cos^{-1}x$$

$$\frac{dy}{dx} = \frac{-1}{\sqrt{1-x^2}}$$

2. Find the derivative of $\sin^{-1}3x$

Solution

$$y = \sin^{-1}3x$$

Let us use the chain rule to solve this problem

Let $u = 3x$

Hence, $y = \sin^{-1}u$

$$\frac{du}{dx} = 3$$

$$\frac{dy}{du} = \frac{1}{\sqrt{1-u^2}}$$

Therefore, $\dfrac{dy}{dx} = \dfrac{dy}{du} \times \dfrac{du}{dx}$ (Chain rule)

$$= \frac{1}{\sqrt{1-u^2}} \times 3$$

$$= \frac{3}{\sqrt{1-u^2}}$$

$$= \frac{3}{\sqrt{1-(3x)^2}} \qquad \text{(Since } u = 3x)$$

$$\frac{dy}{dx} = \frac{3}{\sqrt{1-9x^2}}$$

3. Find the derivative of $\cot^{-1}x^2$

Solution

$$y = \cot^{-1}x^2$$

Let $u = x^2$

Hence, $y = \cot^{-1}u$

$$\frac{du}{dx} = 2x$$

$$\frac{dy}{du} = \frac{-1}{1+u^2}$$

Therefore, $\dfrac{dy}{dx} = \dfrac{dy}{du} \times \dfrac{du}{dx}$

$$= \frac{-1}{1+u^2} \times 2x$$

$$= \frac{-2x}{1+u^2}$$

$$= \frac{-2x}{1+(x^2)^2} \qquad \text{(since } u = x^2)$$

$$\frac{dy}{dx} = \frac{-2x}{1+x^4}$$

4. If $y = \sec^{-1}2x^3$, find $y = \dfrac{dy}{dx}$

Solution

$$y = \sec^{-1}2x^3$$

Let $u = 2x^3$

Hence, $y = \sec^{-1}u$

$$\frac{du}{dx} = 6x^2$$

$$\frac{dy}{du} = \frac{1}{u\sqrt{u^2-1}}$$

Therefore, $\dfrac{dy}{dx} = \dfrac{dy}{du} \times \dfrac{du}{dx}$

$$= \frac{1}{u\sqrt{u^2 - 1}} \times 6x^2$$

$$= \frac{6x^2}{u\sqrt{u^2 - 1}}$$

$$= \frac{6x^2}{2x^3\sqrt{(2x^3)^2 - 1}} \quad \text{(since } u = 2x^3\text{)}$$

$$\frac{dy}{dx} = \frac{3}{x\sqrt{4x^6 - 1}} \quad \text{(Note that } \frac{6x^2}{2x^3} = \frac{3}{x}\text{)}$$

5. Find the derivative $x^2\tan^{-1}x$

Solution

$$y = x^2\tan^{-1}x$$

we apply the product rule as follows:

$$u = x^2$$

$$v = \tan^{-1}x$$

$$\frac{du}{dx} = 2x$$

$$\frac{dv}{dx} = \frac{1}{1 + x^2}$$

$$\frac{dy}{dx} = u\frac{dv}{dx} + v\frac{du}{dx} \quad \text{(product rule)}$$

$$= x^2\left(\frac{1}{1 + x^2}\right) + \tan^{-1}x(2x)$$

$$\frac{dy}{dx} = \frac{x^2}{1 + x^2} + 2x\tan^{-1}x$$

6. If $y = 3x - 1 \cosec^{-1}x^3$, find $\frac{dy}{dx}$.

Solution

$$y = 3x - 1 \cosec^{-1}x^3$$

$$u = 3x - 1$$

$$\frac{du}{dx} = 3$$

$$v = \cosec^{-1}x^3$$

$$\frac{dv}{dx} = \frac{-1}{x^3\sqrt{(x^3)^2 - 1}} \times 3x^2 \quad \text{(From use of chain rule. Note that } 3x^2 \text{ is from the derivative of } x^3\text{)}$$

$$= \frac{-3x^2}{x^3\sqrt{x^6 - 1}}$$

$$\frac{dv}{dx} = \frac{-3}{x\sqrt{x^6 - 1}}$$

$$\frac{dy}{dx} = u\frac{dv}{dx} + v\frac{du}{dx} \quad \text{(product rule)}$$

$$= 3x - 1\left(\frac{-3}{x\sqrt{x^6 - 1}}\right) + \cosec^{-1}x^3(3)$$

$$\frac{dy}{dx} = \frac{-3(3x - 1)}{x\sqrt{x^6 - 1}} + 3\cosec^{-1}x^3$$

7. Find the derivative of $\cos^{-1}(5x - 3)$

<u>Solution</u>

$$y = \cos^{-1}(5x - 3)$$

Let $u = 5x - 3$

Hence, $y = \cos^{-1}u$

$$\frac{du}{dx} = 5$$

$$\frac{dy}{du} = \frac{-1}{\sqrt{1 - u^2}}$$

Therefore, $\dfrac{dy}{dx} = \dfrac{dy}{du} \times \dfrac{du}{dx}$

$$= \frac{-1}{\sqrt{1 - u^2}} \times 5$$

$$= \frac{-5}{\sqrt{1 - u^2}}$$

$$= \frac{-5}{\sqrt{1 - (5x - 3)^2}} \qquad \text{(Since } u = 5x - 3\text{)}$$

Expanding the bracket gives:

$$\frac{dy}{dx} = \frac{-5}{\sqrt{1 - (25x^2 - 15x - 15x + 9)}}$$

$$= \frac{-5}{\sqrt{1 - 25x^2 + 15x + 15x - 9}}$$

$$\frac{dy}{dx} = \frac{-5}{\sqrt{-25x^2 + 30x - 8}}$$

8. If $y = \tan^{-1}\left(\dfrac{1}{m}\right)$, find $\dfrac{dy}{dm}$

<u>Solution</u>

$$y = \tan^{-1}\left(\frac{1}{m}\right)$$

Let $u = \dfrac{1}{m} = m^{-1}$

Hence, $y = \tan^{-1}u$

$$\frac{du}{dm} = -1m^{-2}$$

$$\frac{du}{dm} = \frac{-1}{m^2}$$

$$\frac{dy}{du} = \frac{1}{1 + u^2}$$

Therefore, $\dfrac{dy}{dm} = \dfrac{dy}{du} \times \dfrac{du}{dm}$

$$= \dfrac{1}{1+u^2} \times \dfrac{-1}{m^2}$$

$$= \dfrac{1}{1+\left(\dfrac{1}{m}\right)^2} \times \dfrac{-1}{m^2}$$

$$= \dfrac{-1}{m^2\left[1+\left(\dfrac{1}{m}\right)^2\right]}$$

$$= \dfrac{-1}{m^2\left(1+\dfrac{1}{m^2}\right)}$$

$$\dfrac{dy}{dm} = \dfrac{-1}{m^2+1}$$

9. If $y = \sin 3x$, find $\dfrac{dx}{dy}$.

Solution

$y = \sin 3x$

$\sin^{-1}y = 3x$ (Recall that if $\sin a = b$, then $a = \sin^{-1}b$)

$x = \dfrac{\sin^{-1}y}{3}$

$x = \dfrac{1}{3}\sin^{-1}y$

Hence, $\dfrac{dx}{dy} = \dfrac{1}{3}\dfrac{1}{\sqrt{1-y^2}}$

$$\dfrac{dx}{dy} = \dfrac{1}{3\sqrt{1-y^2}}$$

Note that this example asked us to find $\dfrac{dx}{dy}$ and not $\dfrac{dy}{dx}$

10. If $y = (\cos 5x)^2$ find $\dfrac{dx}{dy}$.

Solution

$y = (\cos 5x)^2$

This can also be written as $\cos^2 5x$. Hence:

$y = \cos^2 5x$.

Or, $\cos^2 5x = y$

taking the square root of both sides gives:

$\cos 5x = \sqrt{y}$

$5x = \cos^{-1}\sqrt{y}$

$$x = \frac{\cos^{-1}\sqrt{y}}{5}$$

$$= \frac{1}{5}\cos^{-1}\sqrt{y}$$

$$x = \frac{1}{5}\cos^{-1}y^{\frac{1}{2}}$$

Hence, $\dfrac{dx}{dy} = \dfrac{1}{5} \cdot \dfrac{-1}{\sqrt{1-(y^{\frac{1}{2}})^2}} \times \dfrac{1}{2}y^{-\frac{1}{2}}$ (Note that $\frac{1}{2}y^{-\frac{1}{2}}$ is from the derivative of $y^{\frac{1}{2}}$)

$$= \frac{-1}{5\sqrt{1-y}} \times \frac{1}{2y^{\frac{1}{2}}}$$

$$= \frac{-1}{10y^{\frac{1}{2}}\sqrt{1-y}}$$

$$= \frac{-1}{10\sqrt{y}\sqrt{1-y}}$$

$$\frac{dx}{dy} = \frac{-1}{10\sqrt{y(1-y)}}$$

Exercise 10

1. If $y = \sin^{-1}2x$ find the $\dfrac{dy}{dx}$.

2. Find the derivative of $\cos^{-1}x$

3. Find the derivative of $\cot^{-1}3x^2$

4. If $y = \cot^{-1}x^4$, find $y = \dfrac{dy}{dx}$

5. Find the derivative $3x\sec^{-1}x$

6. If $y = x^2 + 3\tan^{-1}x$, find $\dfrac{dy}{dx}$.

7. Find the derivative of $\tan^{-1}(x + 5)$

8. If $y = \cos^{-1}\left(\dfrac{1}{x}\right)$, find $\dfrac{dy}{dx}$

9. If $y = \cos5x$, find $\dfrac{dx}{dy}$.

10. If $y = (\sec x)^2$ find $\dfrac{dx}{dy}$.

11. Find the derivative $5x\tan^{-1}3x$

12. If $y = x^2 + 4\sin^{-1}x^5$, find $\dfrac{dy}{dx}$.

13. Find the derivative of $\csc^{-1}x^3$

14. If y = tan2x, find $\dfrac{\mathrm{d}x}{\mathrm{d}y}$.

15. If y = sin^{3}5x, find $\dfrac{\mathrm{d}x}{\mathrm{d}y}$.

CHAPTER 11
DERIVATIVES OF HYPERBOLIC FUNCTIONS

Hyperbolic functions are functions in calculus which are expressed by the combination of the exponential functions e^x and e^{-x}. The derivatives of the six main hyperbolic functions are as given below.

1. If $y = \sinh x$, then $\dfrac{dy}{dx} = \cosh x$

2. If $y = \cosh x$, then $\dfrac{dy}{dx} = \sinh x$

3. If $y = \tanh x$, then $\dfrac{dy}{dx} = \operatorname{sech}^2 x$

4. If $y = \coth x$, then $\dfrac{dy}{dx} = -\operatorname{cosech}^2 x$

5. If $y = \operatorname{sech} x$, then $\dfrac{dy}{dx} = -\operatorname{sech} x \tanh x$

6. If $y = \operatorname{cosech} x$, then $\dfrac{dy}{dx} = -\operatorname{cosech} x \coth x$

Note that $\sinh x = \dfrac{e^x - e^{-x}}{2}$ and $\cosh x = \dfrac{e^x + e^{-x}}{2}$

Examples

1. If $y = \cosh x - 5\sinh x$, find $\dfrac{dy}{dx}$.

Solution

$\quad y = \cosh x - 5\sinh x$

$\quad \dfrac{dy}{dx} = \sinh x - 5\cosh x$

2. Find the derivative of $2x^3 \coth x$

Solution

$\quad y = 2x^3 \coth x$

Using product rule gives $\dfrac{dy}{dx}$ as follows:

$\dfrac{dy}{dx} = 2x^3 \left[\dfrac{d(\coth x)}{dx} \right] + \coth x \left[\dfrac{d(2x^3)}{dx} \right]$

$\quad = 2x^3(-\operatorname{cosech}^2 x) + \coth x(6x^2)$

$\quad = -2x^3 \operatorname{cosech}^2 x + 6x^2 \coth x$

$\dfrac{dy}{dx} = -2x^2(x\operatorname{cosech}^2 x - 3\coth x)$

Take note of the change in sign of the term in the bracket. This is due to the negative sign outside the bracket. Expanding the bracket gives the original expression that was factorized.

3. If $y = \dfrac{\cosh x}{x^2 + 1}$ find $\dfrac{dy}{dx}$.

Solution

Let us use product rule to obtained $\dfrac{dy}{dx}$ as follows:

$$\frac{dy}{dx} = \frac{(x^2 + 1)\left[\frac{d(\cosh x)}{dx}\right] - \cosh x\left[\frac{d(x^2 + 1)}{dx}\right]}{(x^2 + 1)^2}$$

$$= \frac{(x^2 + 1)(\sinh x) - \cosh x(2x)}{(x^2 + 1)^2}$$

$$\frac{dy}{dx} = \frac{\sinh x(x^2 + 1) - 2x\cosh x}{(x^2 + 1)^2}$$

4. Find the derivative of $(\sinh 3x)^2$

Solution

$y = (\sinh 3x)^2$ (This can also be written as $\sinh^2 3x$)

Let $u = \sinh 3x$

Hence, $y = u^2$

$\dfrac{du}{dx} = 3\cosh 3x$ (Note that 3 is from the derivative of $3x$)

$\dfrac{dy}{du} = 2u$

$\dfrac{dy}{dx} = \dfrac{dy}{du} \times \dfrac{du}{dx}$

$\quad = 2u \times 3\cosh 3x$

$\quad = 6u\cosh 3x$

$\quad = 6\sinh 3x \cosh 3x$ (u has been replaced with $\sinh 3x$)

5. Find the derivative of $\sinh^4 2x^3$

Solution

$y = \sinh^4 2x^3$

Let $u = \sinh 2x^3$

Hence, $y = u^4$

$\dfrac{du}{dx} = 6x^2\cosh 2x^3$ (Note that $6x^2$ is from the derivative of $2x^3$)

$\dfrac{dy}{du} = 4u^3$

$\dfrac{dy}{dx} = \dfrac{dy}{du} \times \dfrac{du}{dx}$

$\quad = 4u^3 \times 6x^2\cosh 2x^3$

$\quad = 24x^2 u^3\cosh 2x^3$

$\dfrac{dy}{dx} = 24x^2\sinh^3 2x^3\cosh 2x^3$ (u has been replaced with $\sinh 2x^3$)

6. Find the derivative of $\text{cosech}4x^3$

Solution

$$y = \text{cosech}4x^3$$

$$\frac{dy}{dx} = -\text{cosech}4x^3\text{coth}4x^3 \ \times \ \frac{d(4x^3)}{dx} \qquad \text{(Note that the derivative of cosech is } -\text{cosechcoth)}$$

$$= -\text{cosech}4x^3\text{coth}4x^3 \ \times \ 12x^2$$

$$= -12x^2\text{cosech}4x^3\text{coth}4x^3$$

7. Find the derivative of $\text{coth}^2 2x^4$

Solution

$$y = \text{coth}^2 2x^4$$

Let $u = \text{coth}2x^4$

Hence, $y = u^2$

$$\frac{du}{dx} = -\text{cosech}^2 2x^4 \ \times \ \frac{d(2x^4)}{dx}$$

$$= -\text{cosech}^2 2x^4 \ \times \ 8x^3$$

$$\frac{du}{dx} = -8x^3\text{cosech}^2 2x^4$$

$$\frac{dy}{du} = 2u$$

Therefore, $\dfrac{dy}{dx} = \dfrac{dy}{du} \ \times \ \dfrac{du}{dx}$

$$= 2u \ \times \ (-8x^3\text{cosech}^2 2x^4)$$

$$= -16x^3 u \ \text{cosech}^2 2x^4$$

$$\frac{dy}{dx} = -16x^3\text{coth}2x^4\text{cosech}^2 2x^4 \qquad \text{(Since } u = \text{coth}2x^4)$$

8. Find the derivative of $5x\sinh2x$

Solution

$$y = 5x\sinh2x$$

We apply the product rule of differentiation as follows:

Let $u = 5x$

and $v = \sinh2x$

$$\frac{du}{dx} = 5$$

$$\frac{dv}{dx} = 2\cosh2x \qquad \text{(Note that the differentiation of } 2x \text{ gives 2)}$$

Hence, $\dfrac{dy}{dx} = u\dfrac{dv}{dx} \ + \ v\dfrac{du}{dx}$

$$= (5x \ \times \ 2\cosh2x) + (\sinh2x \ \times \ 5)$$

$$= 10x\cosh2x \ + \ 5\sinh2x$$

$$\frac{dy}{dx} = 5(2x\cosh2x + \sinh2x)$$

9. If $y = \dfrac{1 + \cosh 2x}{\sinh 2x}$ find $\dfrac{dy}{dx}$.

Solution

$$y = \frac{1 + \cosh 2x}{\sinh 2x}$$

We apply quotient rule as follows:

$u = 1 + \cosh2x$

$v = \sinh2x$

$$\frac{du}{dx} = 2\sinh2x$$

$$\frac{dv}{dx} = 2\cosh2x$$

Hence, $\dfrac{dy}{dx} = \dfrac{v\frac{du}{dx} - u\frac{dv}{dx}}{v^2}$ (Quotient rule)

$$= \frac{\sinh 2x(2\sinh 2x) - (1 + \cosh 2x)(2\cosh 2x)}{(\sinh 2x)^2}$$

$$= \frac{2\sin^2 2x - (2\cosh 2x + 2\cosh^2 2x)}{\sinh^2 2x}$$ (Note that $(\sinh2x)^2 = \sinh^2 2x$)

$$= \frac{2\sinh^2 2x - 2\cosh 2x - 2\cosh^2 2x}{\sinh^2 2x}$$

$$= \frac{2\sinh^2 2x - 2\cosh^2 2x - 2\cosh 2x}{\sinh^2 2x}$$

$$= \frac{-2(\cosh^2 2x - \sinh^2 2x) - 2\cosh 2x}{\sinh^2 2x}$$

$$= \frac{-2(1) - 2\cosh 2x}{\sinh^2 2x}$$ (Note that $\cosh^2 2x - \sinh^2 2x = 1$)

$$\frac{dy}{dx} = \frac{-2(1 + \cosh 2x)}{\sinh^2 2x}$$

Or, $\dfrac{dy}{dx} = \dfrac{-2(1 + \cosh 2x)}{\cosh^2 2x - 1}$ (Note that since $\cosh^2 2x - \sinh^2 2x = 1$, then $\cosh^2 2x - 1 = \sinh^2 2x$)

$$= \frac{-2(1 + \cosh 2x)}{(\cosh 2x + 1)(\cosh 2x - 1)}$$

Note that from difference of two squares we have: $a^2 - b^2 = (a + b)(a - b)$.

Hence, $\cosh^2 2x - 1$ is also a difference of two squares since 1 is also 1^2. Therefore, $\cosh^2 2x - 1 = (\cosh2x + 1)(\cosh2x - 1)$ as represented above. Hence the expression above becomes:

$$\frac{dy}{dx} = \frac{-2}{(\cosh 2x - 1)}$$

10. Differentiate $y = \dfrac{\sinh^2 x}{x}$

<u>Solution</u>

$$y = \frac{\sinh^2 x}{x}$$

We use quotient rule as follows:

Therefore, u = $\sinh^2 x$

$\quad$ v = x

Hence, $\dfrac{du}{dx}$ = 2sinh$x$cosh$x$

Since, v = x

Then, $\dfrac{dv}{dx}$ = 1

Hence, $\dfrac{dy}{dx} = \dfrac{v\frac{du}{dx} - u\frac{dv}{dx}}{v^2}$

$$= \frac{x(2\sinh x\cosh x) - \sinh^2 x(1)}{x^2}$$

$$= \frac{2x\sinh x\cosh x - \sin^2 x}{x^2}$$

$$= \frac{\sinh x(2x\cosh x - \sinh x)}{x^2}$$

Exercise 11

1. If y = sinh3x – 2cosh$x$, find $\dfrac{dy}{dx}$.

2. Find the derivative of $5x^2$sech$x$

3. If y = $\dfrac{\sinh 2x}{3x^2}$ find $\dfrac{dy}{dx}$.

4. Find the derivative of cosh^{2}3x

5. Find the derivative of cosh^{3}4x^5

6. Find the derivative of coth2x^5

7. Find the derivative of (sech2x^2)^3

8. Find the derivative of x^2cosh5x

9. If y = $\dfrac{\tanh 5x}{\coth 3x}$ find $\dfrac{dy}{dx}$.

10. Differentiate y = $\dfrac{2\cosh^3 x}{3x}$

CHAPTER 12
DERIVATIVE OF LOGARITHMIC FUNCTIONS

If y = $\log_a x$, then $\dfrac{dy}{dx} = \dfrac{1}{x} \log_a e$, where a is any base.

If y = $\log_e x$, then $\dfrac{dy}{dx} = \dfrac{1}{x}$

Note that $\log_e x$ can also be represented as $\ln x$ and the value of e is 2.718 (to 3 decimal places)

Examples

1. Find the derivative of $\log_a 2x$.

Solution

$\quad$ y = $\log_a 2x$

We will use chain rule since we have a function that is not just x but $2x$.

Let u = $2x$

Therefore, y = $\log_a u$

$\dfrac{du}{dx} = 2$

$\dfrac{dy}{du} = \dfrac{1}{u} \log_a e$

$\dfrac{dy}{dx} = \dfrac{dy}{du} \times \dfrac{du}{dx}$

$\quad = \dfrac{1}{u} \log_a e \times 2$

$\quad = \dfrac{2}{u} \log_a e$

$\quad = \dfrac{2}{2x} \log_a e \qquad$ (since u = $2x$)

$\dfrac{dy}{dx} = \dfrac{1}{x} \log_a e$

2. Find the derivative of $\log_a(5x - 1)$

<u>Solution</u>

$\quad$ y = $\log_a(5x - 1)$

Let u = $5x - 1$

Therefore, y = $\log_a u$

$\dfrac{du}{dx} = 5$

$\dfrac{dy}{du} = \dfrac{1}{u} \log_a e$

$\dfrac{dy}{dx} = \dfrac{dy}{du} \times \dfrac{du}{dx}$

$$= \frac{1}{u} \log_a e \times 5$$

$$= \frac{5}{u} \log_a e$$

$$\frac{dy}{dx} = \frac{5}{5x-1} \log_a e \qquad \text{(since } u = 5x - 1\text{)}$$

3. Differentiate $\log_a(4x-3)^2$ with respect to x

<u>Solution</u>

$$y = \log_a(4x-3)^2$$

Let $u = (4x-3)^2$

Therefore, $y = \log_a u$

$$\frac{du}{dx} = 2(4x-3)^{2-1} \times 4 \qquad \text{(Note that 4 is from the derivative of } 4x - 3\text{)}$$

$$\frac{du}{dx} = 8(4x-3)$$

$$\frac{dy}{du} = \frac{1}{u} \log_a e$$

$$\frac{dy}{dx} = \frac{dy}{du} \times \frac{du}{dx}$$

$$= \frac{1}{u} \log_a e \times 8(4x-3)$$

$$= \frac{8(4x-3)}{u} \log_a e$$

$$= \frac{8(4x-3)}{(4x-3)^2} \log_a e \qquad \text{[since } u = (4x-3)^2\text{]}$$

$$\frac{dy}{dx} = \frac{8}{4x-3} \log_a e \qquad \text{(One } 4x - 3 \text{ cancels out)}$$

4. If $y = \log_a\sqrt{1 + 2x}$, find $\dfrac{dy}{dx}$

<u>Solution</u>

$$y = \log_a\sqrt{1 + 2x}$$

Let $u = \sqrt{1 + 2x} = (1 + 2x)^{\frac{1}{2}}$

Therefore, $y = \log_a u$

$$\frac{du}{dx} = \frac{1}{2}(1 + 2x)^{\frac{1}{2}-1} \times 2$$

$$= (1 + 2x)^{-\frac{1}{2}} \qquad \text{(Note that } \frac{1}{2} \times 2 = 1\text{)}$$

$$\frac{du}{dx} = \frac{1}{(1+2x)^{\frac{1}{2}}}$$

$$\frac{dy}{du} = \frac{1}{u} \log_a e$$

$$\frac{dy}{dx} = \frac{dy}{du} \times \frac{du}{dx}$$

$$= \frac{1}{u}\log_a e \times \frac{1}{(1+2x)^{\frac{1}{2}}}$$

$$= \frac{1}{(1+2x)^{\frac{1}{2}}}\log_a e \times \frac{1}{(1+2x)^{\frac{1}{2}}} \qquad \text{[Note that u has been replaced with } (1+2x)^{\frac{1}{2}}]$$

$$\frac{dy}{dx} = \frac{1}{1+2x}\log_a e \qquad \text{[Note that } (1+2x)^{\frac{1}{2}} \times (1+2x)^{\frac{1}{2}} = (1+2x)^1 \text{ by adding exponents]}$$

5. Find $\dfrac{dy}{dx}$ given that y = $\log_a\dfrac{1-3x}{1+3x}$

Solution

$$y = \log_a\frac{1-3x}{1+3x}$$

Or, y = $\log_a(1-3x) - \log_a(1+3x)$ (Recall that $\log_x\left(\dfrac{a}{b}\right) = \log_x a - \log_x b$)

$$\frac{dy}{dx} = \frac{-3}{1-3x}\log_a e - \frac{3}{1+3x}\log_a e$$

$$= -\log_a e\left(\frac{3}{1-3x} + \frac{3}{1+3x}\right)$$

$$= -\log_a e\left[\frac{3(1+3x) + 3(1-3x)}{(1-3x)(1+3x)}\right]$$

$$= -\log_a e\left[\frac{3+9x+3-9x}{1-9x^2}\right] \qquad \text{[Note that } (1-3x)(1+3x) = 1-9x^2]$$

$$= -\log_a e\left(\frac{6}{1-9x^2}\right)$$

$$\frac{dy}{dx} = \frac{-6}{1-9x^2}\log_a e$$

6. If y = $\log_{10}(x^2 - 2)$, find $\dfrac{dy}{dx}$.

Solution

$$y = \log_{10}(x^2 - 2)$$

The value 10 represents a in other examples. So we are going to differentiate y like the examples above except that we will write 10 wherever 'a' should be.

$$y = \log_{10}(x^2 - 2)$$
$$u = x^2 - 2$$

Hence, y = $\log_{10}u$

$$\frac{du}{dx} = 2x$$

$$\frac{dy}{du} = \frac{1}{u}\log_{10}e \qquad \text{(Just like differentiating } \log_a u)$$

$$\frac{dy}{dx} = \frac{dy}{du} \times \frac{du}{dx}$$

$$= \frac{1}{u} \log_{10} e \times 2x$$

$$= \frac{2x}{u} \log_{10} e$$

$$\frac{dy}{dx} = \frac{2x}{x^2 - 2} \log_{10} e$$

7. Find $\frac{dy}{dx}$ if $y = \log_{10} \frac{1}{x}$

<u>Solution</u>

$$y = \log_{10} \frac{1}{x}$$

Let us solve this question directly without using $u = \frac{1}{x}$ as follows:

$$\frac{dy}{dx} = \frac{\frac{d\left(\frac{1}{x}\right)}{dx}}{\frac{1}{x}} \times \log_{10} e$$

$$= \frac{\frac{d(x^{-1})}{dx}}{x^{-1}} \times \log_{10} e$$

$$= \frac{-x^{-2}}{x^{-1}} \times \log_{10} e \qquad \text{(Note that the derivative of } x^{-1} \text{ is } -x^{-2})$$

$$= -x^{-2} \times x^1 \times \log_{10} e \qquad \text{(Since } \frac{1}{x^{-1}} = x^1)$$

$$= -x^{-1} \times \log_{10} e \qquad \text{(After adding the exponents of } x)$$

$$\frac{dy}{dx} = -\frac{1}{x} \log_{10} e$$

8. Find the derivative of $\log_e(2 - x^3)$

<u>Solution</u>

$$y = \log_e(2 - x^3)$$

Note that the base here is 'e' and not 'a'.

Let $u = 2 - x^3$

Hence, $y = \log_e u$

$$\frac{du}{dx} = -3x^2$$

$$\frac{dy}{du} = \frac{1}{u} \qquad \text{(Recall that the derivative of } \log_e x = \frac{1}{x})$$

$$\frac{dy}{dx} = \frac{dy}{du} \times \frac{du}{dx}$$

$$= \frac{1}{u} \times -3x^2$$

$$= \frac{-3x^2}{u}$$

$$\frac{dy}{dx} = \frac{-3x^2}{2 - x^3}$$

9. Find the derivative of $(\log_e 5x)^2$

Solution

$y = (\log_e 5x)^2$

Let $u = \log_e 5x$

Hence, $y = u^2$

$$\frac{du}{dx} = \frac{\frac{d(5x)}{dx}}{5x}$$

$$= \frac{5}{5x}$$

$$\frac{du}{dx} = \frac{1}{x}$$

$$\frac{dy}{du} = 2u$$

$$\frac{dy}{dx} = \frac{dy}{du} \times \frac{du}{dx}$$

$$= 2u \times \frac{1}{x}$$

$$= \frac{2u}{x}$$

$$\frac{dy}{dx} = \frac{2}{x} \log_e 5x \quad \text{(Since } u = \log_e 5x\text{)}$$

10. If $y = \ln\sqrt{3x^2 - 4}$, find $\frac{dy}{dx}$.

Solution

$y = \ln\sqrt{3x^2 - 4}$

Note that $\ln\sqrt{3x^2 - 4}$ is also the same as $\log_e\sqrt{3x^2 - 4}$

Hence, $y = \log_e\sqrt{3x^2 - 4}$

Or, $y = \log_e(3x^2 - 4)^{\frac{1}{2}}$

Let $u = (3x^2 - 4)^{\frac{1}{2}}$

Hence, $y = \log_e u$

$$\frac{du}{dx} = \frac{1}{2}(3x^2 - 4)^{\frac{1}{2} - 1} \times 6x \quad \text{(Note that } 6x \text{ is from the derivative of } 3x^2 - 4\text{)}$$

$$= \frac{6x}{2}(3x^2 - 4)^{-\frac{1}{2}}$$

$$\frac{du}{dx} = \frac{3x}{(3x^2 - 4)^{\frac{1}{2}}}$$

$$\frac{dy}{du} = \frac{1}{u}$$

$$\frac{dy}{dx} = \frac{dy}{du} \times \frac{du}{dx}$$

$$= \frac{1}{u} \times \frac{3x}{(3x^2 - 4)^{\frac{1}{2}}}$$

$$= \frac{1}{(3x^2 - 4)^{\frac{1}{2}}} \times \frac{3x}{(3x^2 - 4)^{\frac{1}{2}}}$$

$$\frac{dy}{dx} = \frac{3x}{3x^2 - 4}$$ (Note that $(3x^2 - 4)^{\frac{1}{2}} \times (3x^2 - 4)^{\frac{1}{2}} = 3x^2 - 4$, after adding their exponents)

11. Find $\frac{dy}{dx}$ if $y = \sqrt[3]{x} \, \ln 2x$.

Solution

$y = \sqrt[3]{x} \, \ln 2x$

We are going to apply product rule here.

$u = \sqrt[3]{x} = x^{\frac{1}{3}}$

$v = \ln 2x$ (Note that $\ln 2x$ is the same as $\log_e 2x$)

$$\frac{du}{dx} = \frac{1}{3} x^{\frac{1}{3} - 1}$$

$$= \frac{1}{3} x^{-\frac{2}{3}}$$

$$\frac{dv}{dx} = \frac{2}{2x}$$

$$= \frac{1}{x}$$

Hence, $\frac{dy}{dx} = u\frac{dv}{dx} + v\frac{du}{dx}$ (Product rule)

$$= x^{\frac{1}{3}} \left(\frac{1}{x}\right) + \ln 2x \left(\frac{1}{3} x^{-\frac{2}{3}}\right)$$

$$= x^{\frac{1}{3}} (x^{-1}) + \frac{1}{3} x^{-\frac{2}{3}} \ln 2x$$

$$= x^{-\frac{2}{3}} \left(1 + \frac{\ln 2x}{3}\right)$$

$$= x^{-\frac{2}{3}} \left(\frac{3 + \ln 2x}{3}\right)$$

$$\frac{dy}{dx} = \frac{1}{x^{\frac{2}{3}}} \left(\frac{3 + \ln 2x}{3}\right)$$

Or, $\frac{dy}{dx} = \frac{1}{\sqrt[3]{x^2}} \left(\frac{3 + \ln 2x}{3}\right)$

12. Find $\frac{dy}{dx}$ given that $y = \ln(1 + 2x)^2$

Solution

$y = \ln(1 + 2x)^2$ [Also $y = \log_e(1 + 2x)^2$]

Let $u = (1 + 2x)^2$

Hence, $y = \ln u$

$$\frac{du}{dx} = 2(1 + 2x) \times \frac{d(2x)}{dx}$$

$$= 2(1 + 2x) \times 2x$$

$$\frac{du}{dx} = 4(1 + 2x)$$

$$\frac{dy}{du} = \frac{1}{u}$$

$$\frac{dy}{dx} = \frac{1}{u} \times 4(1 + 2x)$$

$$= \frac{4(1+2x)}{u}$$

$$= \frac{4(1+2x)}{(1+2x)^2}$$

$$= \frac{4}{1+2x}$$

13. Differentiate with respect to x: $5x\ln(3x^2 - 2)$

<u>Solution</u>

$$y = 5x\ln(3x^2 - 2)$$

By using product rule:

$$u = 5x$$

$$v = \ln(3x^2 - 2)$$

$$\frac{du}{dx} = 5$$

$$\frac{dv}{dx} = \frac{6x}{3x^2 - 2}$$

Hence, $\dfrac{dy}{dx} = u\dfrac{dv}{dx} + v\dfrac{du}{dx}$

$$= 5x\left(\frac{6x}{3x^2 - 2}\right) + \ln(3x^2 - 2)(5)$$

$$\frac{dy}{dx} = \frac{30x^2}{3x^2 - 2} + 5\ln(3x^2 - 2)$$

14. Find the derivative of $\dfrac{\ln x}{x}$

<u>Solution</u>

$$y = \frac{\ln x}{x}$$

We are going to use quotient rule as follows:

$$u = \ln x$$

$$v = x$$

$$\frac{du}{dx} = \frac{1}{x}$$

$$\frac{dv}{dx} = 1$$

Hence, $\dfrac{dy}{dx} = \dfrac{v\dfrac{du}{dx} - u\dfrac{dv}{dx}}{v^2}$

$$= \frac{x\left(\frac{1}{x}\right) - \ln x\,(1)}{x^2}$$

$$\frac{dy}{dx} = \frac{1 - \ln x}{x^2}$$

Exercise 12

1. Find the derivative of $\log_a 7x$.

2. Find the derivative of $\log_a(x^3 + 5)$

3. Differentiate $\log_a(2x^3 - 5)^6$ with respect to x

4. If $y = \log_a x^{\frac{2}{3}}$, find $\dfrac{dy}{dx}$

5. Find $\dfrac{dy}{dx}$ given that $y = \log_a \dfrac{1 + x^2}{1 - x^2}$

6. If $y = \log_5(5x^3 - 1)$, find $\dfrac{dy}{dx}$.

7. Find $\dfrac{dy}{dx}$ if $y = \log_2 \dfrac{1}{x^2}$

8. Find the derivative of $\log_e(x^2 + 3)$

9. Find the derivative of $(\log_e x)^3$

10. If $y = \ln\sqrt{1 - 2x^5}$, find $\dfrac{dy}{dx}$.

11. Find $\dfrac{dy}{dx}$ if $y = x^4 \ln x^2$

12. Find $\dfrac{dy}{dx}$ given that $y = \ln(3 - 7x)^4$

13. Differentiate with respect to x: $3x^2 \ln(4x^3 + 1)$

14. Find the derivative of $\dfrac{\ln x^2}{x^2}$

15. Find the derivative of $\log_e(1 - 5x^2)^3$

CHAPTER 13
DERIVATIVE OF EXPONENTIAL FUNCTIONS

If $y = a^x$, then $\dfrac{dy}{dx} = a^x \log_e a$, where 'a' is any number.

If $y = e^x$, then $\dfrac{dy}{dx} = e^x$

Examples

1. Differentiate with respect to x: a^{5x}

Solution

$y = a^{5x}$

Let $u = 5x$

$y = a^u$

$\dfrac{du}{dx} = 5$

$\dfrac{dy}{du} = a^u \log_e a$

Hence, $\dfrac{dy}{dx} = \dfrac{dy}{du} \times \dfrac{du}{dx}$

$= a^u \log_e a \times 5$

$= 5a^u \log_e a$

$\dfrac{dy}{dx} = 5a^{5x} \log_e a$ (since $u = 5x$)

2. Find the derivative of $a^{x^2 - 3x + 4}$

Solution

$y = a^{x^2 - 3x + 4}$

Let us solve this example directly without using $u = x^2 - 3x + 4$

$\dfrac{dy}{dx} = \dfrac{d(x^2 - 3x + 4)}{dx} \times a^{x^2 - 3x + 4} \times \log_e a$

$= (2x - 3)(a^{x^2 - 3x + 4} \times \log_e a)$

3. If $y = 3x^2 a^{5x}$, find $\dfrac{dy}{dx}$.

Solution

$y = 3x^2 a^{5x}$

We apply product rule as follows:

$u = 3x^2$

$v = a^{5x}$

$$\frac{du}{dx} = 6x$$

$$\frac{dv}{dx} = 5a^{5x}\log_e a$$

Hence, $\dfrac{dy}{dx} = u\dfrac{dv}{dx} + v\dfrac{du}{dx}$

$$= 3x^2(5a^{5x}\log_e a) + a^{5x}(6x)$$

$$= 15x^2a^{5x}\log_e a + 6xa^{5x}$$

Factorizing the expression above gives:

$$\frac{dy}{dx} = 3xa^{5x}(5x\log_e a + 2)$$

4. Find the derivative of $\dfrac{e^x + e^{-x}}{e^x - e^{-x}}$

Solution

$$y = \frac{e^x + e^{-x}}{e^x - e^{-x}}$$

$$u = e^x + e^{-x}$$

$$v = e^x - e^{-x}$$

$$\frac{du}{dx} = e^x - e^{-x}$$ (The derivative of $e^{-x} = -1 \times e^{-x} = -e^{-x}$. The value -1 is from the derivative of $-x$)

$$\frac{dv}{dx} = e^x + e^{-x}$$

Hence, $\dfrac{dy}{dx} = \dfrac{v\dfrac{du}{dx} - u\dfrac{dv}{dx}}{v^2}$ (Quotient rule)

$$= \frac{(e^x - e^{-x})(e^x - e^{-x}) - (e^x + e^{-x})(e^x + e^{-x})}{(e^x - e^{-x})^2}$$

Expanding the numerator and denominator gives:

$$\frac{dy}{dx} = \frac{(e^x)(e^x) - (e^x)(e^{-x}) - (e^{-x})(e^x) + (e^{-x})(e^{-x}) - [(e^x)(e^x) + (e^x)(e^{-x}) + (e^{-x})(e^x) + (e^{-x})(e^{-x})]}{(e^x - e^{-x})^2}$$

$$= \frac{e^{2x} - 1 - 1 + e^{-2x} - (e^{2x} + 1 + 1 + e^{-2x})}{(e^x - e^{-x})^2}$$ (Note that exponents have been added, and $e^0 = 1$)

$$= \frac{e^{2x} - 2 + e^{-2x} - e^{2x} - 1 - 1 - e^{-2x})}{(e^x - e^{-x})^2}$$

$$\frac{dy}{dx} = \frac{-4}{(e^x - e^{-x})^2}$$ (e^{2x} and e^{-2x} cancel out)

5. If $y = e^{\sqrt{x}}$ find $\dfrac{dy}{dx}$.

Solution

$$y = e^{\sqrt{x}} = e^{x^{\frac{1}{2}}}$$

106

$$\frac{dy}{dx} = \frac{d(x)^{\frac{1}{2}}}{dx} \times e^{x^{\frac{1}{2}}}$$

$$= \frac{1}{2}x^{-\frac{1}{2}} \times e^{x^{\frac{1}{2}}}$$

$$= \frac{1}{2}\left(\frac{1}{x^{\frac{1}{2}}}\right) \times e^{x^{\frac{1}{2}}}$$

$$= \frac{e^{x^{\frac{1}{2}}}}{2x^{\frac{1}{2}}}$$

$$\frac{dy}{dx} = \frac{e^{\sqrt{x}}}{2\sqrt{x}}$$

6. Find $\frac{dy}{dx}$ if $y = x^{\frac{1}{2}}\, e^{x^{\frac{1}{2}}}$

Solution

$$y = x^{\frac{1}{2}}\, e^{x^{\frac{1}{2}}}$$

From product rule:

$$\frac{dy}{dx} = x^{\frac{1}{2}}\frac{d(e^{x^{\frac{1}{2}}})}{dx} + e^{x^{\frac{1}{2}}}\frac{d(x^{\frac{1}{2}})}{dx}$$

$$= x^{\frac{1}{2}}\left(\frac{e^{x^{\frac{1}{2}}}}{2x^{\frac{1}{2}}}\right) + e^{x^{\frac{1}{2}}}\left(\frac{1}{2}x^{-\frac{1}{2}}\right) \quad \text{(Note that the derivative of } e^{x^{\frac{1}{2}}} \text{ is } \frac{e^{x^{\frac{1}{2}}}}{2x^{\frac{1}{2}}} \text{ from example 5)}$$

$$= \frac{e^{x^{\frac{1}{2}}}}{2} + \frac{e^{x^{\frac{1}{2}}}}{2x^{\frac{1}{2}}}$$

$$= \frac{x^{\frac{1}{2}}e^{x^{\frac{1}{2}}} + e^{x^{\frac{1}{2}}}}{2x^{\frac{1}{2}}}$$

$$\frac{dy}{dx} = \frac{e^{x^{\frac{1}{2}}}(x^{\frac{1}{2}} + 1)}{2x^{\frac{1}{2}}}$$

7. Find the derivative of $a^{2x} - a^{-2x}$

Solution

$$y = a^{2x} - a^{-2x}$$

$$\frac{dy}{dx} = \frac{d(2x)}{dx}(a^{2x}\log_e a) - \left[\frac{d(-2x)}{dx}(a^{-2x}\log_e a)\right]$$

$$= 2a^{2x}\log_e a - (-2a^{-2x}\log_e a)$$

$$= 2a^{2x}\log_e a \; + \; 2a^{-2x}\log_e a$$
$$= 2\log_e a(a^{2x} \; + \; a^{-2x})$$

8. Find the derivative of $e^{2x}\log_e 3x$

Solution

$$y = e^{2x}\log_e 3x$$

By product rule:

$$u = e^{2x}$$
$$v = \log_e 3x \quad (\text{or } v = \ln 3x)$$
$$\frac{du}{dx} = 2e^{2x}$$
$$\frac{dv}{dx} = \frac{3}{3x}$$
$$= \frac{1}{x}$$
$$\frac{dy}{dx} = e^{2x}\left(\frac{1}{x}\right) \; + \; \log_e 3x(2e^{2x})$$
$$= \frac{e^{2x}}{x} \; + \; 2e^{2x}\log_e 3x$$
$$\frac{dy}{dx} = e^{2x}(\frac{1}{x} \; + \; 2\log_e 3x)$$

9. Differentiate with respect to x: $\; 2\sqrt{xe^x}$

Solution

$$y = 2\sqrt{xe^x}$$
Or, $y = 2\sqrt{x} \; \sqrt{e^x}$

From product rule:

$$u = 2\sqrt{x} = 2x^{\frac{1}{2}}$$
$$v = \sqrt{e^x} = (e^x)^{\frac{1}{2}}$$
$$v = e^{\frac{1}{2}x} \quad (\text{When the exponents are multiplied})$$
$$\frac{du}{dx} = \frac{1}{2} \; \times \; 2x^{-\frac{1}{2}}$$
$$= x^{-\frac{1}{2}}$$
$$\frac{dv}{dx} = \frac{1}{2} \; e^{\frac{1}{2}x} \quad (\text{Note that } \frac{1}{2} \text{ is from the derivative of } \frac{1}{2}x)$$
$$\frac{dy}{dx} = u\frac{dv}{dx} + v\frac{du}{dx}$$
$$= 2x^{\frac{1}{2}}(\frac{1}{2} \; e^{\frac{1}{2}x}) \; + \; e^{\frac{1}{2}x}(x^{-\frac{1}{2}})$$

$$= \left(\frac{1}{2} \times 2x^{\frac{1}{2}} \times e^{\frac{1}{2}x}\right) \times \frac{e^{\frac{1}{2}x}}{x^{\frac{1}{2}}}$$

$$= x^{\frac{1}{2}}e^{\frac{1}{2}x} + \frac{e^{\frac{1}{2}x}}{x^{\frac{1}{2}}}$$

$$= \frac{x\,e^{\frac{1}{2}x} + e^{\frac{1}{2}x}}{x^{\frac{1}{2}}}$$

$$= \frac{e^{\frac{1}{2}x}(x+1)}{x^{\frac{1}{2}}}$$

$$= \frac{e^{\frac{x}{2}}(x+1)}{x^{\frac{1}{2}}}$$

$$\frac{dy}{dx} = \frac{\sqrt{e^x}(x+1)}{\sqrt{x}}$$

10. Find the derivative of $2x\log_{10}x$

Solution

$y = 2x\log_{10}x$ (Note that this is similar to $2x\log_a x$)

$u = 2x$

$v = \log_{10}x$

$\dfrac{du}{dx} = 2$

$\dfrac{dv}{dx} = \dfrac{1}{x}\log_{10}e$ (Recall that the derivative of $\log_a x$ is $\dfrac{1}{x}\log_a e$)

$\dfrac{dy}{dx} = u\dfrac{dv}{dx} + v\dfrac{du}{dx}$

$\quad = 2x\left(\dfrac{1}{x}\log_{10}e\right) + \log_{10}x(2)$

$\quad = 2\log_{10}e + 2\log_{10}x$

$\dfrac{dy}{dx} = 2(\log_{10}e + \log_{10}x)$

Or, $\dfrac{dy}{dx} = 2\left(\dfrac{\log_e e}{\log_e 10} + \log_{10}x\right)$

Note that the rule of change of base in logarithm that has been applied above is given by:

If $\log_a b$ is to be converted to a new base, e, then: $\log_a b = \dfrac{\log_e b}{\log_e a}$

$\dfrac{dy}{dx} = 2\left(\dfrac{1}{\log_e 10} + \log_{10}x\right)$ (Recall that $\log_x x = 1$, or $\log_e e = 1$)

11. Find the derivative of 10^{2x}

Solution

109

$$y = 10^{2x} \quad \text{(This is similar to } a^{2x}\text{)}$$

$$\frac{dy}{dx} = \frac{d(2x)}{dx} \times 10^{2x} \log_e 10$$

$$= 2 \times 10^{2x} \log_e 10$$

$$= (10^{2x})2\log_e 10$$

$$= 10^{2x} \log_e 10^2 \quad \text{(Recall that } a\log_x y = \log_x y^a\text{)}$$

$$\frac{dy}{dx} = 10^{2x} \log_e 100$$

12. If $y = e^{\ln x}$ find $\dfrac{dy}{dx}$

<u>Solution</u>

$$y = e^{\ln x} \quad \text{(Or } y = e^{\log_e x} \text{ since } \ln x = \log_e x\text{)}$$

Let, $u = \ln x$

$$y = e^u$$

$$\frac{du}{dx} = \frac{1}{x}$$

$$\frac{dy}{du} = e^u$$

$$\frac{dy}{dx} = e^u \times \frac{1}{x}$$

$$= \frac{e^u}{x}$$

$$= \frac{e^{\ln x}}{x} \quad \text{(Since } u = \ln x\text{)}$$

$$= \frac{e^{\log_e x}}{x} \quad \text{(Since } \ln x = \log_e x\text{)}$$

$$= \frac{x}{x} \quad \text{(Recall the identity that } m^{\log_m n} = n\text{)}$$

$$\frac{dy}{dx} = 1$$

This example shows that calculus works, since the derivative of x is 1, and the derivative of $e^{\log_e x} = 1$ because $e^{\log_e x} = x$. Hence, we could have solved this example by stating that:

$$\frac{d(e^{\ln x})}{dx} = \frac{d(x)}{dx} = 1$$

13. What is the derivative of $\dfrac{e^{\frac{1}{x}}}{x^2}$

<u>Solution</u>

$$y = \frac{e^{\frac{1}{x}}}{x^2}$$

From quotient rule:

110

$$u = e^{\frac{1}{x}}$$

$$v = x^2$$

$$\frac{du}{dx} = \frac{d\left(\frac{1}{x}\right)}{dx} \times e^{\frac{1}{x}}$$

$$= \frac{d(x^{-1})}{dx} \times e^{\frac{1}{x}}$$

$$= -1x^{-2} \times e^{\frac{1}{x}}$$

$$= \frac{-1}{x^2} \times e^{\frac{1}{x}}$$

$$\frac{du}{dx} = \frac{-e^{\frac{1}{x}}}{x^2}$$

$$\frac{du}{dx} = 2x$$

$$\frac{dy}{dx} = \frac{v\frac{du}{dx} - u\frac{dv}{dx}}{v^2} \qquad \text{(Quotient rule)}$$

$$= \frac{x^2\left(\frac{-e^{\frac{1}{x}}}{x^2}\right) - e^{\frac{1}{x}}(2x)}{(x^2)^2}$$

$$= \frac{-e^{\frac{1}{x}} - 2x\,e^{\frac{1}{x}}}{x^4} \qquad \text{(Note that } x^2 \text{ has cancelled out)}$$

14. Find the derivative of $e^{-5x} + 5e$

Solution

$$y = e^{-5x} + 5e$$

$$\frac{dy}{dx} = \frac{d(-5x)}{dx} \times e^{-5x} + \frac{d(5e)}{dx}$$

$$= -5e^{-5x} + 0 \qquad \text{(Note that 5e is a constant and the derivative of a constant is zero)}$$

$$\frac{dy}{dx} = -5e^{-5x}$$

15. If $y = e^{(2x+3)^2}$ find $\frac{dy}{dx}$.

Solution

$$y = e^{(2x+3)^2}$$

Let $u = (2x + 3)^2$

Hence, $y = e^u$

$$\frac{du}{dx} = 2(2x + 3)^{2-1} \times \frac{d(2x)}{dx} \qquad \text{(Using chain rule)}$$

$$= 2(2x + 3) \times 2$$

$$= 4(2x + 3)$$

$$\frac{dy}{du} = e^u$$

$$\frac{dy}{dx} = \frac{dy}{du} \times \frac{du}{dx}$$

$$= e^u \times 4(2x + 3)$$

$$= e^{(2x+3)^2} \times 4(2x + 3) \qquad \text{(Note that } u = (2x + 3)^2)$$

$$\frac{dy}{dx} = 4(2x + 3)e^{(2x+3)^2}$$

16. Differentiate with respect to θ, $5^{2\theta}$

<u>Solution</u>

$$y = 5^{2\theta} \qquad \text{(This is like } y = a^{2\theta})$$

$$\frac{dy}{d\theta} = \frac{d(2\theta)}{d\theta} \times 5^{2\theta} \log_e 5$$

$$= 2 \times 5^{2\theta} \log_e 5$$

$$= (5^{2\theta})2\log_e 5$$

$$= 5^{2\theta} \log_e 5^2 \qquad \text{(Note that } 2\log_e 5 = \log_e 5^2)$$

$$\frac{dy}{d\theta} = 5^{2\theta} \log_e 25$$

Exercise 13

1. Differentiate with respect to x: $5a^{2x}$

2. Find the derivative of $a^{5x^3 - x}$

3. If $y = x^4 a^{3x}$, find $\frac{dy}{dx}$.

4. Find the derivative of $\frac{3 + e^{-x}}{e^x}$

5. If $y = 2e^{\sqrt{3x}}$ find $\frac{dy}{dx}$.

6. Find $\frac{dy}{dx}$ if $y = 6x^3 e^{x^2}$

7. Find the derivative of $a^{-5x} + a^{5x}$

8. Find the derivative of $3e^{4x}\log_e 2x^2$

9. Differentiate with respect to x: $3x^2\sqrt{e^{5x}}$

10. Find the derivative of $x^4 \log_{10} 7x$

11. Find the derivative of 6^{3x}

12. Find the derivative of $e^{x^2 - 3x}$

13. What is the derivative of $\dfrac{2e^{\frac{3}{x}}}{10x^5}$

14. Find the derivative of $1 - 2e^{-3x}$

15. If $y = e^{(x^2+x)^3}$ find $\dfrac{dy}{dx}$.

16. Differentiate with respect to x, 2^{x^2}

17. Find the derivative of $\dfrac{a^x - a^{-x}}{a^{-x}}$

18. Find the derivative of $e^x \ln 10x^3$

19. Differentiate with respect to x: $e^{2x}\sqrt{5x}$

20. Find the derivative of $2x^5 \log_{10} 5x^4$

CHAPTER 14
LOGARITHMIC DIFFERENTIATION

A function of x could be raised to an exponent which is also a function of x. An example is x^x.

The differentiation of such a function is called logarithmic differentiation.

This type of function is differentiated by first taking the logarithm of both sides of the equation, and then differentiating implicitly before making $\dfrac{dy}{dx}$ the subject of the formula (i.e. solving for $\dfrac{dy}{dx}$). Finally, y (i.e. the function) is substituted into the final answer.

Examples

1. Find the derivative of x^x.

<u>Solution</u>

$$y = x^x$$

This is a function of x raised to an exponent which is also a function of x.

Hence, take the logarithm to base e of both sides as follows:

$$\log_e y = \log_e x^x$$
$$\log_e y = x\log_e x \quad \text{(Note that } \log_m n^b = b\log_m n\text{)}$$

Now differentiate y implicitly and differentiate the right hand side using product rule. This gives:

$$\frac{1}{y}\frac{dy}{dx} = x\frac{1}{x} + \log_e x(1) \quad \text{(Use of product rule on the right hand side, with u = } x \text{ and v = } \log_e x\text{)}$$

$$\frac{1}{y}\frac{dy}{dx} = 1 + \log_e x$$

Multiply both sides by y to make $\dfrac{dy}{dx}$ the subject of the formula as follows:

$$\frac{dy}{dx} = y(1 + \log_e x)$$

$$\frac{dy}{dx} = x^x(1 + \log_e x) \quad \text{(Since y = } x^x\text{)}$$

2. Find the derivative of $x^{\ln x}$.

<u>Solution</u>

$$y = x^{\ln x}$$

Taking the logarithm of both sides gives:

$$\log_e y = \log_e x^{\ln x}$$
$$\log_e y = \ln x\log_e x$$

Differentiate y implicitly and treat the right hand side using product rule as follows:

$$\frac{1}{y}\frac{dy}{dx} = \ln x\left(\frac{1}{x}\right) + \log_e x\left(\frac{1}{x}\right)$$

114

$$\frac{1}{y}\frac{dy}{dx} = \left(\frac{\ln x}{x}\right) + \left(\frac{\ln x}{x}\right)$$ (Note that $\log_e x$ can also be written as $\ln x$)

$$\frac{1}{y}\frac{dy}{dx} = \frac{2\ln x}{x}$$

Multiply both sides by y. This gives:

$$\frac{dy}{dx} = y\left(\frac{2\ln x}{x}\right)$$

$$\frac{dy}{dx} = x^{\ln x}\left(\frac{2\ln x}{x}\right)$$ (Since $y = x^{\ln x}$)

Or, $\dfrac{dy}{dx} = \dfrac{2}{x}x^{\ln x}\ln x$

3. If $y = \ln(2 + x)^x$ find $\dfrac{dy}{dx}$.

<u>Solution</u>

$y = \ln(2 + x)^x$

In this case we are not going to take the logarithm of both sides since there is already logarithm on the right hand side. Hence, we proceed as follows:

$y = \ln(2 + x)^x$

$y = x\log_e(2 + x)$ [Note that $\ln(2 + x)$ can also be written as $\log_e(2 + x)$]

Using product rule gives:

$$\frac{dy}{dx} = x\left(\frac{1}{2 + x}\right) + \log_e(2 + x)(1)$$

$$\frac{dy}{dx} = \frac{x}{2 + x} + \log_e(2 + x)$$

4. Find $\dfrac{dy}{dx}$ if $y = (x^2 - 3)^{5x}$

<u>Solution</u>

$y = (x^2 - 3)^{5x}$

Taking the natural logarithm of both sides gives:

$\log_e y = \log_e(x^2 - 3)^{5x}$

$\log_e y = 5x\log_e(x^2 - 3)$

Using implicit differentiation for the left hand side and product rule for the right hand side gives:

$$\frac{1}{y}\frac{dy}{dx} = 5x\left(\frac{2x}{x^2 - 3}\right) + \log_e(x^2 - 3)(5)$$

$$\frac{1}{y}\frac{dy}{dx} = \frac{10x^2}{x^2 - 3} + 5\log_e(x^2 - 3)$$

Multiply both sides by y to obtain:

$$\frac{dy}{dx} = y\left[\frac{10x^2}{x^2 - 3} + 5\log_e(x^2 - 3)\right]$$

$$\frac{dy}{dx} = (x^2 - 3)^{5x}\left[\frac{10x^2}{x^2 - 3} + 5\log_e(x^2 - 3)\right] \qquad \text{[Note that } y = (x^2 - 3)^{5x}]$$

5. If $y = \dfrac{(x^2 - 5)(3x - 1)^2}{x^7(2x^3 - 3)}$

Solution

This is not a function of x raised to an exponent which is also a function of x. This function can be differentiated by the use of product and quotient rule. However, the use of these rules will be a nightmare. Hence, we have to apply logarithmic differentiation. This is done as follows:

$$y = \frac{(x^2 - 5)(3x - 1)^2}{x^7(2x^3 - 3)}$$

Taking the logarithm of both sides gives:

$$\log_e y = \log_e\left[\frac{(x^2 - 5)(3x - 1)^2}{x^7(2x^3 - 3)}\right]$$

In order to continue, we have to recall the theory of logarithm as follows:

1. $\log_b(cd) = \log_b c + \log_b d$

2. $\log_b\left(\dfrac{c}{d}\right) = \log_b c - \log_b d$

3. $\log_b c^d = d\log_b c$

Therefore, we continue the logarithmic differentiation as follows:

$$\log_e y = \log_e\left[\frac{(x^2 - 5)(3x - 1)^2}{x^7(2x^3 - 3)}\right]$$

Applying the theory above gives:

$$\log_e y = \log_e[(x^2 - 5)(3x - 1)^2] - \log_e[x^7(2x^3 - 3)]$$
$$\log_e y = \log_e(x^2 - 5) + \log_e(3x - 1)^2 - [\log_e x^7 + \log_e(2x^3 - 3)]$$
$$\log_e y = \log_e(x^2 - 5) + 2\log_e(3x - 1) - 7\log_e x - \log_e(2x^3 - 3)$$

Differentiating each term accordingly gives:

$$\frac{1}{y}\frac{dy}{dx} = \frac{2x}{x^2 - 5} + \frac{2 \times 3}{3x - 1} - \frac{7}{x} - \frac{6x}{2x^3 - 3}$$

Note that each function of x is differentiated first, and the value obtained is then divided by the original function. Hence, the expression above simplifies to gives:

$$\frac{1}{y}\frac{dy}{dx} = \frac{2x}{x^2 - 5} + \frac{6}{3x - 1} - \frac{7}{x} - \frac{6x}{2x^3 - 3}$$

Multiply both sides by y to obtain $\dfrac{dy}{dx}$ as follows:

$$\frac{dy}{dx} = y\left(\frac{2x}{x^2 - 5} + \frac{6}{3x - 1} - \frac{7}{x} - \frac{6x}{2x^3 - 3}\right)$$

Now replace y with its original value from the question as follows:

$$\frac{dy}{dx} = \left[\frac{(x^2 - 5)(3x - 1)^2}{x^7(2x^3 - 3)}\right]\left(\frac{2x}{x^2 - 5} + \frac{6}{3x - 1} - \frac{7}{x} - \frac{6x}{2x^3 - 3}\right)$$

6. If $y = \dfrac{(2x - 1)(x + 4)(6x - 5)}{(3 - x)^2}$

Solution

$$y = \frac{(2x - 1)(x + 4)(6x - 5)}{(3 - x)^2}$$

This is a complex function where product rule and quotient rule would be difficult to apply.

Hence, we apply logarithmic differentiation as follows:

$$\log_e y = \log_e\left[\frac{(2x - 1)(x + 4)(6x - 5)}{(3 - x)^2}\right]$$

Applying the theory of logarithm gives:

$$\log_e y = \log_e[(2x - 1)(x + 4)(6x - 5)] - \log_e(3 - x)^2$$
$$\log_e y = \log_e(2x - 1) + \log_e(x + 4) + \log_e(6x - 5) - 2\log_e(3 - x)$$

Differentiating accordingly gives:

$$\frac{1}{y}\frac{dy}{dx} = \frac{2}{2x - 1} + \frac{1}{x + 4} + \frac{6}{6x - 5} - \frac{2(-1)}{3 - x}$$

$$\frac{1}{y}\frac{dy}{dx} = \frac{2}{2x - 1} + \frac{1}{x + 4} + \frac{6}{6x - 5} + \frac{2}{3 - x}$$

Multiply both sides by y. This gives:

$$\frac{dy}{dx} = y\left(\frac{2}{2x - 1} + \frac{1}{x + 4} + \frac{6}{6x - 5} + \frac{2}{3 - x}\right)$$

Finally replace y with its original expression as follows:

$$\frac{dy}{dx} = \left[\frac{(2x - 1)(x + 4)(6x - 5)}{(3 - x)^2}\right]\left(\frac{2}{2x - 1} + \frac{1}{x + 4} + \frac{6}{6x - 5} + \frac{2}{3 - x}\right)$$

7. Find the derivative of x^{x^2}

Solution

$$y = x^{x^2}$$
$$\log_e y = \log_e x^{x^2}$$
$$\log_e y = x^2\log_e x$$
$$\frac{1}{y}\frac{dy}{dx} = x^2\left(\frac{1}{x}\right) + \log_e x(2x)$$
$$\frac{1}{y}\frac{dy}{dx} = x + 2x\log_e x$$
$$\frac{1}{y}\frac{dy}{dx} = x(1 + 2\log_e x)$$
$$\frac{dy}{dx} = yx(1 + 2\log_e x)$$
$$= x^{x^2}x(1 + 2\log_e x) \qquad \text{(y has been replaced with } x^{x^2}\text{)}$$
$$\frac{dy}{dx} = x^{x^2 + 1}(1 + 2\log_e x)$$

Note that the exponents of x^{x^2} and x were added to obtain $x^{x^2 + 1}$ since x is also x^1

8. If $y = e^{e^x}$ find $\dfrac{dy}{dx}$.

Solution

$$y = e^{e^x}$$

$$\log_e y = \log_e e^{e^x}$$

$$\log_e y = e^x \log_e e$$

$$\log_e y = e^x \qquad \text{(Recall that logarithm of a number to the same base is 1. Hence, } \log_e e = 1)$$

$$\frac{1}{y}\frac{dy}{dx} = e^x \qquad \text{(Note that the derivative of } e^x \text{ is } e^x)$$

$$\frac{dy}{dx} = ye^x$$

$$= e^{e^x} e^x$$

$$\frac{dy}{dx} = e^{e^x + x} \qquad \text{(Their exponents have been added)}$$

9. Find the derivative of 5^{2^x}

Solution

$$y = 5^{2^x}$$

$$\log_e y = \log_e 5^{2^x}$$

$$\log_e y = 2^x \log_e 5$$

Differentiate the left hand side implicitly. On the right hand side, differentiate 2^x and take $\log_e 5$ as a constant. This gives:

$$\frac{1}{y}\frac{dy}{dx} = 2^x \log_e 2 \log_e 5$$

Note that 2^x is treated in a similar way as a^x, and recall that the derivative of a^x is $a^x \log_e a$. Hence the derivative of 2^x is $2^x \log_e 2$, and $\log_e 5$ multiplies it since it is a constant. Therefore:

$$\frac{dy}{dx} = y(2^x \log_e 2 \log_e 5)$$

$$= 5^{2^x}(2^x \log_e 2 \log_e 5)$$

$$\frac{dy}{dx} = 5^{2^x}(2^x \log_e 2)(\log_e 5)$$

10. If $y = x^{\ln(2x^2 - 5)}$, find $\dfrac{dy}{dx}$.

Solution

$$y = x^{\ln(2x^2 - 5)}$$

$$\log_e y = \log_e x^{\ln(2x^2 - 5)}$$

$$\log_e y = \ln(2x^2 - 5)\log_e x$$

$$\frac{1}{y}\frac{dy}{dx} = \ln(2x^2 - 5)\left(\frac{1}{x}\right) + \log_e x \left(\frac{4x}{2x^2 - 5}\right) \qquad \text{(Use of product rule)}$$

118

$$\frac{1}{y}\frac{dy}{dx} = \frac{1}{x}\ln(2x^2 - 5) + \left(\frac{4x}{2x^2-5}\right)\log_e x$$

$$\frac{dy}{dx} = y\left[\frac{1}{x}\ln(2x^2 - 5) + \left(\frac{4x}{2x^2-5}\right)\log_e x\right]$$

$$\frac{dy}{dx} = x^{\ln(2x^2-5)}\left[\frac{\ln(2x^2-5)}{x} + \left(\frac{4x}{2x^2-5}\right)\log_e x\right]$$

Exercise 14

1. Find the derivative of x^{2x}

2. Find the derivative of $3x^{\ln 2x}$.

3. If $y = \ln(1 - 4x^2)^x$ find $\frac{dy}{dx}$.

4. Find $\frac{dy}{dx}$ if $y = (6x^2 - 5)^{3x}$

5. If $y = \frac{(2x^3 + 1)(x - 2)^3}{3x^2(x^3 - 1)^2}$

6. If $y = \frac{(2x - 1)(x^2 - 2)}{(1 - x)(x - 3)^2}$

7. Find the derivative of $5x^{3x^4}$

8. If $y = e^{e^{3x}}$ find $\frac{dy}{dx}$.

9. Find the derivative of 2^{e^x}

10. If $y = x^{\ln(x^2 - 4x)}$, find $\frac{dy}{dx}$.

11. If $y = \ln(10 + 2x^2)^x$ find $\frac{dy}{dx}$.

12. Find $\frac{dy}{dx}$ if $y = (3x^3 - 8)^{2x}$

13. If $y = \frac{(x + 3)^2(x - 3)^2}{(x^3 - 1)}$

14. If $y = 5x^{(\ln x)^2}$, find $\frac{dy}{dx}$.

15. Find the derivative of $10x^{3x^2}$

CHAPTER 15
DERIVATIVE OF ONE FUNCTION WITH RESPECT TO ANOTHER

We can differentiate one function with respect to another as illustrated by the examples shown below.

Examples

1. Differentiate x^{12} with respect to x^7.

Solution

Let $u = x^{12}$

And $v = x^7$

$$\frac{du}{dx} = 12x^{11}$$

$$\frac{dv}{dx} = 7x^6$$

Differentiating x^{12} with respect to x^7 means differentiating u (i.e. x^{12}) with respect to v (i.e. x^7).

This means $\frac{du}{dv}$. This follows the parametric equation rule given by:

$$\frac{du}{dv} = \frac{\frac{du}{dx}}{\frac{dv}{dx}}$$

$$= \frac{12x^{11}}{7x^6}$$

$$= \frac{12}{7}x^5$$

2. Differentiate $2e^x$ with respect to $\ln 2x$.

Solution

The differentiation of $2e^x$ with respect to $\ln 2x$ simply means:

$$\frac{\text{The derivative of } 2e^x}{\text{The derivative of } \ln 2x}$$

Hence, $\frac{d(2e^x)}{dx} = 2e^x$

And, $\frac{d(\ln 2x)}{dx} = \frac{2}{2x} = \frac{1}{x}$

Therefore, the differentiation of $2e^x$ with respect to $\ln 2x$ is given by:

$$\frac{2e^x}{\frac{1}{x}}$$

$$= 2xe^x$$

3. Differntiate $\sin 5x$ with respect to $\cos x$.

Solution

Hence, $\dfrac{d(\sin 5x)}{dx} = 5\cos 5x$

And, $\dfrac{d(\cos x)}{dx} = -\sin x$

Therefore, the differentiation of sin5x with respect to cosx is given by:

$$\dfrac{\text{The derivative of } \sin 5x}{\text{The derivative of } \cos x}$$

$$= \dfrac{5\cos 5x}{-\sin x}$$

$$= -\dfrac{5\cos 5x}{\sin x}$$

4. Find the derivative of $2x^2 - 5$ with respect to $4x - 1$

Solution

This is obtained as follows:

$$\dfrac{\dfrac{d(2x^2 - 5)}{dx}}{\dfrac{d(4x - 1)}{dx}}$$

$$= \dfrac{4x}{4}$$

$$= x$$

Exercise 15

1. Differentiate x^3 with respect to x^5.
2. Differentiate e^{5x} with respect to $\ln x^2$
3. Differentiate $\cos x^2$ with respect to $\sin x$.
4. Find the derivative of $4x^3 - 5x^2$ with respect to $(x - 1)^2$
5. Differentiate $7x^4$ with respect to $3x^2$.
6. Differentiate $2a^x$ with respect to e^x.
7. Differentiate $\tan^2 x$ with respect to $\cos 5x$.
8. Find the derivative of $\ln(x - 1)$ with respect to e^{x-1}
9. Differentiate $\log_e x^5$ with respect to e^{5x}.
10. Differentiate $\ln(e^x - e^{-x})$ with respect to $\ln x^x$

CHAPTER 16
HIGHER DERIVATIVES (SUCCESSIVE DIFFERENTIATION)

If f(x) is differentiated it gives the first derivative denoted by f'(x) or $\frac{dy}{dx}$. If we differentiate f'(x), it gives the second derivative denoted by f''(x) or $\frac{d^2y}{dx^2}$ (read as, dee two y dee x squared). Other higher derivatives such as $\frac{d^3y}{dx^3}, \frac{d^4y}{dx^4}$ etc can also be obtained depending on the function.

Examples

1. Find the first, second and third derivatives of $2x^5 - 3x^4 + 5x^2 - 6$

<u>Solution</u>

$$y = 2x^5 - 3x^4 + 5x^2 - 6$$

$$\frac{dy}{dx} = 10x^4 - 12x^3 + 10x$$

$\frac{d^2y}{dx^2}$ is obtained by differentiating $\frac{dy}{dx}$, which means to differentiate $10x^4 - 12x^3 + 10x$.

Hence, $\frac{d^2y}{dx^2} = 40x^3 - 36x^2 + 10$

$\frac{d^3y}{dx^3}$ is obtained by differentiating $40x^3 - 36x^2 + 10$ as follows:

$$\frac{d^3y}{dx^3} = 120x^2 - 72x$$

In summary, the first derivative $\left(\frac{dy}{dx}\right)$ is $10x^4 - 12x^3 + 10x$, the second derivative $\left(\frac{d^2y}{dx^2}\right)$ is $40x^3 - 36x^2 + 10$, while the third derivative $\left(\frac{d^3y}{dx^3}\right)$ is $120x^2 - 72x$.

2. If $y = \ln x^2$, find $\frac{d^2y}{dx^2}$.

<u>Solution</u>

$$y = \ln x^2$$

$$\frac{dy}{dx} = \frac{2x}{x^2}$$

$$= \frac{2}{x}$$

$$\frac{d^2y}{dx^2} = \frac{d\left(\frac{2}{x}\right)}{dx}$$

$$= \frac{d(2x^{-1})}{dx}$$

$$= -2x^{-2}$$

$$\frac{d^2y}{dx^2} = \frac{-2}{x^2}$$

3. Find $\frac{d^3y}{dx^3}$ given that $y = e^{x^3}$

Solution

$y = e^{x^3}$

$\frac{dy}{dx} = 3x^2 e^{x^3}$ (Note that $3x^2$ is from the derivative of x^3)

We now use product rule to obtain $\frac{d^2y}{dx^2}$ as follows:

$$\frac{d^2y}{dx^2} = 3x^2 \left[\frac{d(e^{x^3})}{dx}\right] + e^{x^3}\left[\frac{d(3x^2)}{dx}\right]$$

$$= 3x^2(3x^2 e^{x^3}) + e^{x^3}(6x)$$

$$= 9x^4 e^{x^3} + 6xe^{x^3}$$

$$\frac{d^2y}{dx^2} = e^{x^3}(9x^4 + 6x)$$

Finally, let us also use product rule to obtain $\frac{d^3y}{dx^3}$ as follows:

$$\frac{d^3y}{dx^3} = e^{x^3}\left[\frac{d(9x^4 + 6x)}{dx}\right] + (9x^4 + 6x)\left[\frac{d(e^{x^3})}{dx}\right]$$

$$= e^{x^3}(36x^3 + 6) + (9x^4 + 6x)(3x^2 e^{x^3})$$

$$= 36x^3 e^{x^3} + 6e^{x^3} + 27x^6 e^{x^3} + 18x^3 e^{x^3}$$

$$= 27x^6 e^{x^3} + 36x^3 e^{x^3} + 18x^3 e^{x^3} + 6e^{x^3}$$

$$= 27x^6 e^{x^3} + 54x^3 e^{x^3} + 6e^{x^3}$$

$$\frac{d^3y}{dx^3} = 3e^{x^3}(9x^6 + 18x^3 + 2)$$

4. If $y = \sin 2x^3$, find the third derivative of y.

Solution

$y = \sin 2x^3$

$\frac{dy}{dx} = \cos 2x^3 \frac{d(2x^3)}{dx}$ (Recall that the derivative of $\sin x$ is $\cos x$)

$= \cos 2x^3 (6x^2)$

$\frac{dy}{dx} = 6x^2 \cos 2x^3$

We now use product rule to obtain $\frac{d^2y}{dx^2}$ as follows:

$$\frac{d^2y}{dx^2} = 6x^2\left[\frac{d(\cos 2x^3)}{dx}\right] + \cos 2x^3\left[\frac{d(6x^2)}{dx}\right]$$

123

$$= 6x^2\left[-\sin 2x^3 \frac{d(2x^3)}{dx}\right] + \cos 2x^3(12x)$$

$$= 6x^2\left[-\sin 2x^3 (6x^2)\right] + 12x\cos 2x^3$$

$$\frac{d^2y}{dx^2} = -36x^4 \sin 2x^3 + 12x\cos 2x^3$$

Again, the use of product rule gives us $\frac{d^3y}{dx^3}$ as follows:

$$\frac{d^3y}{dx^3} = -36x^4\left[\frac{d(\sin 2x^3)}{dx}\right] + \sin 2x^3\left[\frac{d(-36x^4)}{dx}\right] + 12x\left[\frac{d(\cos 2x^3)}{dx}\right] + \cos 2x^3\left[\frac{d(12x)}{dx}\right]$$

Note that the derivative of $\sin 2x^3$ is $6x^2\cos 2x^3$ as obtained from $\frac{dy}{dx}$. Similarly, the differentiation of $\cos 2x^3$ will give us $-6x^2\sin 2x^3$ (since the derivative of $\sin x$ and $\cos x$ differs only by sign and the interchanging of sin with cos or cos with sin).

We now replace the derivative of $\sin 2x^3$ and $\cos 2x^3$ with $6x^2\cos 2x^3$ and $-6x^2\sin 2x^3$ respectively in the expression above. This gives:

$$\frac{d^3y}{dx^3} = -36x^4 (6x^2\cos 2x^3) + \sin 2x^3(-144x^3) + 12x (-6x^2\sin 2x^3) + \cos 2x^3(12)$$

$$= -216x^6\cos 2x^3 - 144x^3\sin 2x^3 - 72x^3\sin 2x^3 + 12\cos 2x^3$$

$$\frac{d^3y}{dx^3} = -216x^6\cos 2x^3 - 216x^3\sin 2x^3 + 12\cos 2x^3$$

Or, $\frac{d^3y}{dx^3} = -12(18x^6\cos 2x^3 + 18x^3\sin 2x^3 - \cos 2x^3)$

5. Find $\frac{d^2y}{dx^2}$ given that $y = a^{x^2} - 5$

<u>Solution</u>

$$y = a^{x^2} - 5$$

$$\frac{dy}{dx} = a^{x^2}\left[\frac{d(x^2)}{dx}\right]\log_e a$$

$$= a^{x^2} (2x)\log_e a$$

$$\frac{dy}{dx} = 2x\, a^{x^2} \log_e a$$

We now use product rule to find $\frac{d^2y}{dx^2}$ as follows:

$$\frac{d^2y}{dx^2} = 2x\left[\frac{d\left(a^{x^2}\log_e a\right)}{dx}\right] + a^{x^2}\log_e a\left[\frac{d(2x)}{dx}\right]$$

$$= 2x\left[\frac{\log_e a\, d\left(a^{x^2}\right)}{dx}\right] + a^{x^2}\log_e a(2)$$

$$= 2x[\log_e a(2xa^{x^2}\log_e a)] + 2a^{x^2}\log_e a$$

$$= 4x^2 a^{x^2} (\log_e a)^2 + 2a^{x^2}\log_e a$$

$$\frac{d^2y}{dx^2} = 2a^{x^2}\log_e a(2x^2\log_e a + 1)$$

6. Find the second derivative of $y = \dfrac{\cos x}{x^3}$

Solution

$$y = \frac{\cos x}{x^3}$$

We use quotient rule as follows:

$$\frac{dy}{dx} = \frac{x^3\frac{d(\cos x)}{dx} - \cos x\frac{d(x^3)}{dx}}{(x^3)^2}$$

$$= \frac{x^3(-\sin x) - \cos x(3x^2)}{x^6}$$

$$\frac{dy}{dx} = \frac{-x^3\sin x - 3x^2\cos x}{x^6}$$

Divide each part by x^6 to separate into fractions as follows:

$$\frac{dy}{dx} = \frac{-x^3\sin x}{x^6} - \frac{3x^2\cos x}{x^6}$$

$$\frac{dy}{dx} = \frac{-\sin x}{x^3} - \frac{3\cos x}{x^4}$$

We now apply quotient rule again as follows:

$$\frac{d^2y}{dx^2} = \frac{x^3\frac{d(-\sin x)}{dx} - (-\sin x)\frac{d(x^3)}{dx}}{(x^3)^2} - \left[\frac{x^4\frac{d(3\cos x)}{dx} - 3\cos x\frac{d(x^4)}{dx}}{(x^4)^2}\right]$$

$$= \frac{x^3(-\cos x) + \sin x\,(3x^2)}{x^6} - \left[\frac{x^4(-3\sin x) - 3\cos x\,(4x^3)}{x^8}\right]$$

$$= \frac{-x^3\cos x + 3x^2\sin x}{x^6} + \frac{3x^4\sin x + 12x^3\cos x}{x^8}$$

Separating into fractions gives:

$$\frac{d^2y}{dx^2} = \frac{-x^3\cos x}{x^6} + \frac{3x^2\sin x}{x^6} + \frac{3x^4\sin x}{x^8} + \frac{12x^3\cos x}{x^8}$$

$$= \frac{-\cos x}{x^3} + \frac{3\sin x}{x^4} + \frac{3\sin x}{x^4} + \frac{12\cos x}{x^5}$$

Combining the fractions again by using x^5 as LCM gives:

$$\frac{d^2y}{dx^2} = \frac{-x^2\cos x + 3x\sin x + 3x\sin x + 12\cos x}{x^5}$$

$$\frac{d^2y}{dx^2} = \frac{6x\sin x + 12\cos x - x^2\cos x}{x^5}$$

7. Find the third derivative of $y = \log_e(1 + 2x)^2$

Solution

$$y = \log_e(1 + 2x)^2$$

$$\frac{dy}{dx} = \frac{2(1+2x)^{2-1} \times \frac{d(2x)}{dx}}{(1+2x)^2}$$ [Note the use of chain rule in finding the derivative of $(1 + 2x)^2$]

$$= \frac{2(1+2x) \times 2}{(1+2x)^2}$$

$$= \frac{4(1+2x)}{(1+2x)^2}$$

$$= \frac{4}{1+2x} \qquad (1 + 2x \text{ cancels out})$$

$$\frac{dy}{dx} = 4(1 + 2x)^{-1}$$

Using chain rule gives $\frac{d^2y}{dx^2}$ as follows:

$$\frac{d^2y}{dx^2} = -1 \times 4(1 + 2x)^{-1-1} \times \frac{d(2x)}{dx}$$

$$= -4(1 + 2x)^{-2} \times 2$$

$$= -8(1 + 2x)^{-2}$$

Use of chain rule again gives $\frac{d^3y}{dx^3}$ as follows:

$$\frac{d^3y}{dx^3} = -2 \times -8(1 + 2x)^{-2-1} \times \frac{d(2x)}{dx}$$

$$= 16(1 + 2x)^{-3} \times 2$$

$$= 32(1 + 2x)^{-3}$$

$$\frac{d^3y}{dx^3} = \frac{32}{(1+2x)^3}$$

8. If y = sec2x, find $\frac{d^3y}{dx^3}$.

Solution

$$y = \sec 2x$$

$$\frac{dy}{dx} = 2\sec 2x \tan 2x$$

We now use product rule to obtain $\frac{d^2y}{dx^2}$ as follows:

$$\frac{d^2y}{dx^2} = 2\sec 2x \frac{d(\tan 2x)}{dx} + \tan 2x \frac{d(2\sec 2x)}{dx}$$

$$= 2\sec 2x(2\sec^2 2x) + \tan 2x(2 \times 2 \sec 2x \tan 2x)$$

$$\frac{d^2y}{dx^2} = 4\sec^3 2x + 4\sec 2x \tan^2 2x$$

We now use chain rule for $4\sec^3 2x$ and product rule for $4\sec 2x \tan^2 2x$ to obtain $\frac{d^3y}{dx^3}$ as follows:

$$\frac{d^3y}{dx^3} = 3 \times 4 \sec^2 2x \frac{d(\sec 2x)}{dx} + 4\sec 2x \frac{d(\tan^2 2x)}{dx} + \tan^2 2x \frac{d(4\sec 2x)}{dx}$$

$$= 12\sec^2 2x(2\sec 2x \tan 2x) + 4\sec 2x \left[2\tan 2x \frac{d(\tan 2x)}{dx}\right] + \tan^2 2x[4(2\sec 2x \tan 2x)]$$

126

$= 24\sec^3 2x\tan 2x + 8\sec 2x\tan 2x(2\sec^2 2x) + 8\sec 2x\tan^3 2x$

$= 24\sec^3 2x\tan 2x + 16\sec^3 2x\tan 2x + 8\sec 2x\tan^3 2x$

$\dfrac{d^3 y}{dx^3} = 40\sec^3 2x\tan 2x + 8\sec 2x\tan^3 2x$

9. Given that y = 2cos5x + 3sin5x, prove that $\dfrac{d^2 y}{dx^2}$ + 25y = 0

Solution

  y = 2cos5x + 3sin5x

  $\dfrac{dy}{dx}$ = 2 x 5(−sin5x) + 3 x 5(cos5x)

   = −10sin5x + 15cos5x

  $\dfrac{d^2 y}{dx^2}$ = −10 x 5(cos5x) + 15 x 5(−sin5x)

   = −50cos5x − 75sin5x

We now obtain 25y as follows:

  y = 2cos5x + 3sin5x

25y = 25(2cos5x + 3sin5x)

25y = 50cos5x + 75sin5x

We now simplify $\dfrac{d^2 y}{dx^2}$ + 25y as follows:

  $\dfrac{d^2 y}{dx^2}$ + 25y = −50cos5x − 75sin5x + 50cos5x + 75sin5x

    = 0   (Equal terms with opposite signs cancel out)

Therefore, $\dfrac{d^2 y}{dx^2}$ + 25y = 0   (As proven above)

10. If $y = x + \sqrt{4 + x^2}$, show that $(4 + x^2)\dfrac{d^2 y}{dx^2} + x\dfrac{dy}{dx} - y = 0$

Solution

  $y = x + \sqrt{4 + x^2}$

  $y = x + (4 + x^2)^{\frac{1}{2}}$

  $\dfrac{dy}{dx} = 1 + \dfrac{1}{2}(4 + x^2)^{\frac{1}{2} - 1} \times \dfrac{d(x^2)}{dx}$

   $= 1 + \dfrac{1}{2}(4 + x^2)^{-\frac{1}{2}} \times 2x$

  $\dfrac{dy}{dx} = 1 + x(4 + x^2)^{-\frac{1}{2}}$

Using product rule, we obtain $\dfrac{d^2 y}{dx^2}$ as follows:

$$\frac{d^2y}{dx^2} = 0 + x\left[\frac{d(4+x^2)^{-\frac{1}{2}}}{dx}\right] + (4+x^2)^{-\frac{1}{2}}\frac{d(x)}{dx}$$

$$= x\left[-\frac{1}{2}(4+x^2)^{-\frac{1}{2}-1}\frac{d(x^2)}{dx}\right] + (4+x^2)^{-\frac{1}{2}}(1)$$

$$= x\left[-\frac{1}{2}(4+x^2)^{-\frac{3}{2}} \times 2x\right] + (4+x^2)^{-\frac{1}{2}}$$

$$= -x^2(4+x^2)^{-\frac{3}{2}} + (4+x^2)^{-\frac{1}{2}}$$

$$\frac{d^2y}{dx^2} = \frac{-x^2}{(4+x^2)^{\frac{3}{2}}} + \frac{1}{(4+x^2)^{\frac{1}{2}}}$$

Let us now simplify $(4+x^2)\frac{d^2y}{dx^2} + x\frac{dy}{dx} - y$ as follows:

$$(4+x^2)\left[\frac{-x^2}{(4+x^2)^{\frac{3}{2}}} + \frac{1}{(4+x^2)^{\frac{1}{2}}}\right] + x[1 + x(4+x^2)^{-\frac{1}{2}}] - [x + (4+x^2)^{\frac{1}{2}}]$$

Expanding the brackets gives:

$$-x^2(4+x^2)^{1-\frac{3}{2}} + (4+x^2)^{1-\frac{1}{2}} + x + x^2(4+x^2)^{-\frac{1}{2}} - x - (4+x^2)^{\frac{1}{2}}$$

$$= -x^2(4+x^2)^{-\frac{1}{2}} + (4+x^2)^{\frac{1}{2}} + x + x^2(4+x^2)^{-\frac{1}{2}} - x - (4+x^2)^{\frac{1}{2}}$$

$$= 0 \quad \text{(Note that equal terms with opposite signs cancel out one another to give zero)}$$

Therefore, $(4+x^2)\frac{d^2y}{dx^2} + x\frac{dy}{dx} - y = 0$ (As proven above)

Exercise 16

1. Find the first, second and third derivatives of $x^4 - 2x^3 - 7x^2 + 1$

2. If $y = \ln 2x^3$, find $\frac{d^2y}{dx^2}$.

3. Find $\frac{d^2y}{dx^2}$ given that $y = e^{5x^4}$

4. If $y = \sin^2 x^5$, find the second derivative of y.

5. Find $\frac{d^3y}{dx^3}$ given that $y = \ln(4x - 10)$

6. Find the second derivative of $y = \frac{\sin x}{x}$

7. Find the third derivative of $y = (\ln x)^2$

8. If $y = \cot x$, find $\frac{d^3y}{dx^3}$.

9. Given that $y = \sin^2 x + \cos 2x$, find $\frac{d^2y}{dx^2} - y$

10. If $y = 2e^{2x} + 5e^{-x}$ evaluate $\dfrac{d^2y}{dx^2} - \dfrac{dy}{dx} - 2y$

11. Given that $y = \cos^2x + 2\sin x^2$ find $\dfrac{d^2y}{dx^2} - \dfrac{dy}{dx}$

12. Find the second derivative of $y = \dfrac{\tan x}{3x}$

13. If $y = e^{-x}\cos 2x$, find the second derivative of y.

14. If $y = 2\cos 3x + 5\sin 3x$, evaluate $\dfrac{d^2y}{dx^2} + 9y$

15. Find the second derivative of $y = \dfrac{\sin 3x}{3x}$

CHAPTER 17
MISCELLANEOUS PROBLEMS ON DIFFERENTIAL CALCULUS

This chapter covers worked examples on general problems involving combination of topics treated in the various previous chapters. More challenging problems would also be covered here.

Examples

1. If $y = \dfrac{1}{(2x^3 - 5)^4}$ find $\dfrac{dy}{dx}$.

Solution

$$y = \frac{1}{(2x^3 - 5)^4}$$

This can be written as:

$$y = (2x^3 - 5)^{-4}$$

We now use chain rule to differentiate it as follows:

$$\frac{dy}{dx} = -4(2x^3 - 5)^{-4-1} \times \frac{d(2x^3 - 5)}{dx}$$

$$= -4(2x^3 - 5)^{-5} \times 6x^2$$

$$= -24x^2(2x^3 - 5)^{-5}$$

$$\frac{dy}{dx} = \frac{-24x^2}{(2x^3 - 5)^5}$$

2. Given that $f(x) = 5x^4 - 3x^3 - 7x^2 + 9$, find $f'(2)$

Solution

$$f(x) = 5x^4 - 3x^3 - 7x^2 + 9$$

We differentiate $f(x)$ to obtain $f'(x)$ as follows:

$$f'(x) = 20x^3 - 9x^2 - 14x$$

In order to find $f'(2)$, we simply substitute 2 for x in $f'(x)$ as follows:

$$f'(x) = 20x^3 - 9x^2 - 14x$$

$$f'(2) = 20(2^3) - 9(2^2) - 14(2)$$

$$= 20(8) - 9(4) - 28$$

$$= 160 - 36 - 28$$

$$f'(2) = 96$$

3. A function $f(x)$ is given by $f(x) = \dfrac{\sqrt{4 + 3x^2}}{x^3}$. Find:

(a) the derivative of $f(x)$

(b) the gradient of $f(x)$ at the point $(2, \dfrac{1}{2})$

Solution

(a) $f(x) = \dfrac{\sqrt{4 + 3x^2}}{x^3}$

We apply quotient rule to differentiate $f(x)$ as follows:

$$f'(x) = \frac{x^3\left[\dfrac{d(\sqrt{4+3x^2})}{dx}\right] - \sqrt{4+3x^2}\left[\dfrac{d(x^3)}{dx}\right]}{(x^3)^2}$$

$$= \frac{x^3\left[\dfrac{d(4+3x^2)^{\frac{1}{2}}}{dx}\right] - (4+3x^2)^{\frac{1}{2}}(3x^2)}{x^6}$$

$$= \frac{x^3\left[\dfrac{1}{2}(4+3x^2)^{\frac{1}{2}-1} \times \dfrac{d(3x^2)}{dx}\right] - 3x^2(4+3x^2)^{\frac{1}{2}}}{x^6}$$

$$= \frac{x^3\left[\dfrac{1}{2}(4+3x^2)^{-\frac{1}{2}} \times 6x\right] - 3x^2(4+3x^2)^{\frac{1}{2}}}{x^6}$$

$$= \frac{x^3\left[3x\,(4+3x^2)^{-\frac{1}{2}}\right] - 3x^2(4+3x^2)^{\frac{1}{2}}}{x^6}$$

$$= \frac{3x^4(4+3x^2)^{-\frac{1}{2}} - 3x^2(4+3x^2)^{\frac{1}{2}}}{x^6}$$

Let us factorize the expression above by taking $3x^2(4+3x^2)^{-\frac{1}{2}}$ as the common factor. This gives:

$$f'(x) = \frac{3x^2(4+3x^2)^{-\frac{1}{2}}[x^2 - (4+3x^2)]}{x^6}$$

Note that $(4+3x^2)^{\frac{1}{2}} \div (4+3x^2)^{-\frac{1}{2}} = (4+3x^2)^{\frac{1}{2}-(-\frac{1}{2})} = 4+3x^2$ as the exponent becomes 1. Recall that exponents are subtracted during division.

$$= \frac{3x^2(4+3x^2)^{-\frac{1}{2}}(x^2 - 4 - 3x^2)}{x^6}$$

$$= \frac{3x^2(4+3x^2)^{-\frac{1}{2}}(-2x^2 - 4)}{x^6}$$

$$= \frac{-3x^2(4+3x^2)^{-\frac{1}{2}}(2x^2 + 4)}{x^6}$$

$$= \frac{-3(4+3x^2)^{-\frac{1}{2}}(2x^2 + 4)}{x^4} \qquad \text{(Note that } x^2 \text{ has cancelled out of } x^6\text{)}$$

$$f'(x) = \frac{-3(2x^2 + 4)}{x^4(4+3x^2)^{\frac{1}{2}}}$$

(b) The gradient of f(x) at the point $(2, \frac{1}{2})$ is obtained by substituting 2 for x in f'(x). Note that

the point $(2, \frac{1}{2})$ is at $x = 2$ and $y = \frac{1}{2}$. We ignore $y = \frac{1}{2}$ since y is not in the expression for f'(x).

Hence, $f'(x) = \dfrac{-3(2x^2 + 4)}{x^4(4 + 3x^2)^{\frac{1}{2}}}$

At $(2, \frac{1}{2})$, $f'(2) = \dfrac{-3(2(2)^2 + 4)}{(2)^4(4 + 3(2)^2)^{\frac{1}{2}}}$

$= \dfrac{-3(8 + 4)}{16(4 + 12)^{\frac{1}{2}}}$

$= \dfrac{-3(12)}{16(16)^{\frac{1}{2}}}$

$= \dfrac{-36}{16 \times 4}$ (Note that $(16)^{\frac{1}{2}} = \sqrt{16} = 4$)

$f'(2) = \dfrac{-9}{16}$ (In its lowest term)

Therefore the gradient of f(x) at the point $(2, \frac{1}{2})$ is $\dfrac{-9}{16}$

4. If $x^2y^2 - 3xy + 4xy^3 = 4$, find:
(a) the derivative of the expression
(b) the gradient at $(-1, 2)$

Solution

(a) $x^2y^2 - 3xy + 4xy^3 = 4$

The use of implicit differentiation combined with product rule gives us the derivative as follows:

$$x^2\frac{d(y^2)}{dx} + y^2\frac{d(x^2)}{dx} - \left[3x\frac{d(y)}{dx} + y\frac{d(3x)}{dx}\right] + 4x\frac{d(y^3)}{dx} + y^3(4) = \frac{d(4)}{dx}$$

$$x^2\left(2y\frac{dy}{dx}\right) + y^2(2x) - \left[3x\frac{dy}{dx} + y(3)\right] + 4x\left(3y^2\frac{dy}{dx}\right) + 4y^3 = 0$$

$$2x^2y\frac{dy}{dx} + 2xy^2 - 3x\frac{dy}{dx} - 3y + 12xy^2\frac{dy}{dx} + 4y^3 = 0$$

Collect terms in $\frac{dy}{dx}$ on one side of the equation. This gives:

$$2x^2y\frac{dy}{dx} - 3x\frac{dy}{dx} + 12xy^2\frac{dy}{dx} = 3y - 2xy^2 - 4y^3$$

Factorizing the left hand side gives:

$$\frac{dy}{dx}(2x^2y - 3x + 12xy^2) = 3y - 2xy^2 - 4y^3$$

Divide both sides by the terms in the bracket. This gives:

$$\frac{dy}{dx} = \frac{3y - 2xy^2 - 4y^3}{12x^2y - 3x + 12xy^2}$$

(b) At the point (−1, 2) the gradient of the expression is obtained by simply substituting −1 for x and 2 for y in the expression for the derivative. This is done as follows:

$$\frac{dy}{dx} = \frac{3y - 2xy^2 - 4y^3}{12x^2y - 3x + 12xy^2}$$

$$= \frac{3(2) - 2(-1)(2)^2 - 4(2)^3}{12(-1)^2(2) - 3(-1) + 12(-1)(2)^2}$$

$$= \frac{6 + 8 - 32}{24 + 3 - 48}$$

$$= \frac{-18}{-21}$$

$$= \frac{6}{7}$$

5. Find the derivative of $(x + 3y^2)^3 = 7$

Solution

$(x + 3y^2)^3 = 7$

We differentiate implicitly and apply chain rule as follows:

$$3(x + 3y^2)^{3-1} \times \frac{d(x+3y^2)}{dx} = 0$$

$$3(x + 3y^2)^2\left(1 + 6y\frac{dy}{dx}\right) = 0$$

Dividing both sides by $3(x + 3y^2)^2$ gives:

$$1 + 6y\frac{dy}{dx} = 0 \qquad \left(\text{Note that } \frac{0}{3(x + 3y^2)^2} = 0\right)$$

$$6y\frac{dy}{dx} = -1$$

$$\frac{dy}{dx} = -\frac{1}{6y}$$

6. If y = $(3x^2 - 2x + 5)(2x - 3)$, find $\frac{dy}{dx}$.

Solution

y = $(3x^2 - 2x + 5)(2x - 3)$

We differentiate the expression by applying product rule as follows:

$$\frac{dy}{dx} = (3x^2 - 2x + 5)(2) + (2x - 3)(6x - 2)$$

$$= 6x^2 - 4x + 10 + 12x^2 - 4x - 18x + 6$$

$$\frac{dy}{dx} = 18x^2 - 26x + 16$$

7. Find the derivative of $a^{1 + \tan x}$

Solution

$y = a^{1 + \tan x}$

134

Let u = 1 + tan$x$

Hence, y = a^u

$$\frac{du}{dx} = \sec^2 x$$

$$\frac{dy}{du} = a^u \log_e a$$

Hence, $\frac{dy}{dx} = \frac{dy}{du} \times \frac{du}{dx}$

$$= a^u \log_e a \times \sec^2 x$$

$$\frac{dy}{dx} = a^{1+\tan x} \sec^2 x \log_e a$$

8. Find the derivative of $\frac{\log_e x}{1+\cos x}$

Solution

$$y = \frac{\log_e x}{1+\cos x}$$

We apply product rule as follows:

$$\frac{dy}{dx} = \frac{(1+\cos x)\frac{d(\log_e x)}{dx} - \log_e x \frac{d(1+\cos x)}{dx}}{(1+\cos x)^2}$$

$$= \frac{(1+\cos x)\frac{1}{x} - \log_e x(-\sin x)}{(1+\cos x)^2}$$

$$= \frac{\frac{1+\cos x}{x} + \sin x \log_e x}{(1+\cos x)^2}$$

$$= \frac{\frac{1+\cos x + x\sin x \log_e x}{x}}{(1+\cos x)^2}$$

$$\frac{dy}{dx} = \frac{1+\cos x + x\sin x \log_e x}{x(1+\cos x)^2}$$

9. Differentiate with respect to x: ln(cos$x$ + sin$x$)

Solution

$$y = \ln(\cos x + \sin x)$$

$$\frac{dy}{dx} = \frac{\frac{d(\cos x + \sin x)}{dx}}{\cos x + \sin x}$$

$$= \frac{-\sin x + \cos x}{\cos x + \sin x}$$

$$\frac{dy}{dx} = \frac{\cos x - \sin x}{\cos x + \sin x}$$

10. If $y = e^{\sin 2x + \cos x}$ find $\dfrac{dy}{dx}$.

Solution

$$y = e^{\sin 2x + \cos x}$$

$$\frac{dy}{dx} = \frac{d(\sin 2x + \cos x)}{dx} \times e^{\sin 2x + \cos x}$$

$$= (2\cos 2x - \sin x)(e^{\sin 2x + \cos x})$$

11. Given that $y = e^x - e^{-x}$ show that $\dfrac{d^3y}{dx^3} + \dfrac{d^2y}{dx^2} + \dfrac{dy}{dx} + y = 4e^x$

Solution

$$y = e^x - e^{-x}$$

$$\frac{dy}{dx} = e^x - (-e^{-x}) \qquad \left(\text{Note that } \frac{d(e^{-x})}{dx} = \frac{d(-x)}{dx} \times e^{-x} = -1 \times e^{-x} = -e^{-x}\right)$$

$$= e^x + e^{-x}$$

$$\frac{d^2y}{dx^2} = e^x - e^{-x}$$

$$\frac{d^3y}{dx^3} = e^x + e^{-x}$$

Let us now substitute corresponding term into $\dfrac{d^3y}{dx^3} + \dfrac{d^2y}{dx^2} + \dfrac{dy}{dx} + y$ as follows:

$$(e^x + e^{-x}) + (e^x - e^{-x}) + (e^x + e^{-x}) + (e^x - e^{-x})$$

Collecting like terms together gives:

$$e^x + e^x + e^x + e^x + e^{-x} - e^{-x} + e^{-x} - e^{-x}$$

$$= 4e^x \qquad \text{(Note that } e^{-x} \text{ cancels out each other)}$$

Hence, $\dfrac{d^3y}{dx^3} + \dfrac{d^2y}{dx^2} + \dfrac{dy}{dx} + y = 4e^x$ (As proven above)

12. Differentiate with respect to x: $\ln\left(\dfrac{1 - 3x^2}{1 + 3x^2}\right)^{\frac{1}{2}}$

Solution

$$y = \ln\left(\frac{1 - 3x^2}{1 + 3x^2}\right)^{\frac{1}{2}}$$

$$= \log_e\left(\frac{1 - 3x^2}{1 + 3x^2}\right)^{\frac{1}{2}} \qquad \text{(Note that "ln" is } \log_e\text{)}$$

$$= \log_e\left[\frac{(1 - 3x^2)^{\frac{1}{2}}}{(1 + 3x^2)^{\frac{1}{2}}}\right]$$

$$= \log_e(1 - 3x^2)^{\frac{1}{2}} - \log_e(1 + 3x^2)^{\frac{1}{2}}$$

$$y = \frac{1}{2}\log_e(1 - 3x^2) - \frac{1}{2}\log_e(1 + 3x^2)$$

$$\frac{dy}{dx} = \frac{1}{2}\frac{\frac{d(1-3x^2)}{dx}}{1-3x^2} - \frac{1}{2}\frac{\frac{d(1+3x^2)}{dx}}{1+3x^2}$$

$$= \frac{1}{2}\frac{-6x}{1-3x^2} - \frac{1}{2}\frac{6x}{1+3x^2}$$

$$= \frac{-3x}{1-3x^2} - \frac{3x}{1+3x^2} \qquad \text{(Note that } \frac{1}{2} \text{ reduces } 6x \text{ to } 3x\text{)}$$

$$= \frac{-3x(1+3x^2) - 3x(1-3x^2)}{(1-3x^2)(1+3x^2)}$$

$$= \frac{-3x - 9x^3 - 3x + 9x^3)}{(1-3x^2)(1+3x^2)}$$

$$= \frac{-6x}{1 + 3x^2 - 3x^2 - 9x^4}$$

$$\frac{dy}{dx} = \frac{-6x}{1 - 9x^4}$$

13. If $y = \dfrac{x}{\sqrt{9 - x^2}}$ show that: $(9 - x^2)\dfrac{d^2y}{dx^2} = 3x\dfrac{dy}{dx}$

Solution

$$y = \frac{x}{\sqrt{9 - x^2}}$$

Applying quotient rule gives $\dfrac{dy}{dx}$ as follows:

$$\frac{dy}{dx} = \frac{\sqrt{9 - x^2}(1) - x\frac{d(\sqrt{9 - x^2})}{dx}}{(\sqrt{9 - x^2})^2}$$

$$= \frac{(9 - x^2)^{\frac{1}{2}}(1) - x\frac{d[(9 - x^2)^{\frac{1}{2}}]}{dx}}{[(9 - x^2)^{\frac{1}{2}}]^2}$$

$$= \frac{(9 - x^2)^{\frac{1}{2}} - x\left[\frac{1}{2}(9 - x^2)^{\frac{1}{2} - 1}\right] \times (-2x)}{9 - x^2} \qquad \text{(Note that } -2x \text{ is from the derivative of } -x^2\text{)}$$

$$= \frac{(9 - x^2)^{\frac{1}{2}} - x\left[-x(9 - x^2)^{-\frac{1}{2}}\right]}{9 - x^2}$$

$$= \frac{(9 - x^2)^{\frac{1}{2}} + x^2(9 - x^2)^{-\frac{1}{2}}}{9 - x^2}$$

$$= \frac{(9 - x^2)^{\frac{1}{2}} + \dfrac{x^2}{(9 - x^2)^{\frac{1}{2}}}}{9 - x^2}$$

$$= \frac{\dfrac{9 - x^2 + x^2}{(9-x^2)^{\frac{1}{2}}}}{9 - x^2}$$

$$= \frac{9}{(9-x^2)^{\frac{1}{2}}(9-x^2)}$$

$$= \frac{9}{(9-x^2)^{\frac{3}{2}}}$$

$$\frac{dy}{dx} = 9(9 - x^2)^{-\frac{3}{2}}$$

Applying chain rule gives $\dfrac{d^2y}{dx^2}$ as follows:

$$\frac{d^2y}{dx^2} = \frac{-3}{2} \times 9(9 - x^2)^{-\frac{3}{2} - 1} \times -2x \qquad \text{(Note that } -2x \text{ is from the derivative of } -x^2\text{)}$$

$$= \frac{-27}{2} \times -2x(9 - x^2)^{-\frac{5}{2}}$$

$$= 27x(9 - x^2)^{-\frac{5}{2}}$$

$$\frac{d^2y}{dx^2} = \frac{27x}{(9-x^2)^{\frac{5}{2}}}$$

Let us now show that $(9 - x^2)\dfrac{d^2y}{dx^2} = 3x\dfrac{dy}{dx}$

We simplify $(9 - x^2)\dfrac{d^2y}{dx^2}$ as follows:

$$(9 - x^2)\frac{27x}{(9-x^2)^{\frac{5}{2}}}$$

$$= \frac{27x(9 - x^2)}{(9-x^2)^{\frac{5}{2}}}$$

$$= 27x(9 - x^2)^{1 - \frac{5}{2}}$$

$$= 27x(9 - x^2)^{-\frac{3}{2}}$$

$$= \frac{27x}{(9-x^2)^{\frac{3}{2}}}$$

Hence $(9 - x^2)\dfrac{d^2y}{dx^2}$ gives us $\dfrac{27x}{(9-x^2)^{\frac{3}{2}}}$

Let us now simplify $3x\dfrac{dy}{dx}$ as follows:

$$3x[9(9 - x^2)^{-\frac{3}{2}}] \qquad \text{(Note that } \frac{dy}{dx} = 9(9 - x^2)^{-\frac{3}{2}} \text{ as obtained above)}$$

$$= 27x(9 - x^2)^{-\frac{3}{2}}$$

$$= \frac{27x}{(9-x^2)^{\frac{3}{2}}}$$

Hence $3x\dfrac{dy}{dx}$ also gives us $\dfrac{27x}{(9-x^2)^{\frac{3}{2}}}$

Therefore, $(9-x^2)\dfrac{d^2y}{dx^2} = 3x\dfrac{dy}{dx}$ as both sides give $\dfrac{27x}{(9-x^2)^{\frac{3}{2}}}$

14. Given that $y = \dfrac{x}{x-1}$, show that: $(x-1)\dfrac{d^2y}{dx^2} + 2\dfrac{dy}{dx} = 0$

Solution

$$y = \dfrac{x}{x-1}$$

Using quotient rule gives $\dfrac{dy}{dx}$ as follows:

$$\dfrac{dy}{dx} = \dfrac{(x-1)(1) - x(1)}{(x-1)^2}$$

$$= \dfrac{x-1-x}{(x-1)^2}$$

$$\dfrac{dy}{dx} = \dfrac{-1}{(x-1)^2}$$

Using chain rule gives $\dfrac{d^2y}{dx^2}$ as follows:

$$\dfrac{dy}{dx} = \dfrac{-1}{(x-1)^2}$$

$$= -1(x-1)^{-2}$$

$$\dfrac{d^2y}{dx^2} = -2 \times -1(x-1)^{-2-1} \times \dfrac{d(x)}{dx}$$

$$= 2(x-1)^{-3} \times 1$$

$$\dfrac{d^2y}{dx^2} = \dfrac{2}{(x-1)^3}$$

From the question, let us now simplify $(x-1)\dfrac{d^2y}{dx^2} + 2\dfrac{dy}{dx}$ as follows:

$$(x-1)\dfrac{d^2y}{dx^2} + 2\dfrac{dy}{dx}$$

$$= (x-1)\dfrac{2}{(x-1)^3} + (2)\dfrac{-1}{(x-1)^2}$$

$$= \dfrac{2}{(x-1)^2} - \dfrac{2}{(x-1)^2}$$

$$= 0$$

This shows that $(x-1)\dfrac{d^2y}{dx^2} + 2\dfrac{dy}{dx}$ is equal to zero.

15. Find, with respect to x, the derivative of $\left(x - \dfrac{5}{x}\right)^3$

Solution

$$y = \left(x - \frac{5}{x}\right)^3$$

This can also be written as:

$$y = (x - 5x^{-1})^3$$

$$\frac{dy}{dx} = 3(x - 5x^{-1})^{3-1} \times \frac{d(x - 5x^{-1})}{dx} \qquad \text{(By use of chain rule)}$$

$$= 3(x - 5x^{-1})^2 \times 1 - (-1 \times 5x^{-1-1})$$

$$= 3(x - 5x^{-1})^2 \times 1 - (-5x^{-2})$$

$$= 3(x - 5x^{-1})^2 \times (1 + 5x^{-2})$$

$$= 3(x - 5x^{-1})^2(1 + 5x^{-2})$$

$$\frac{dy}{dx} = 3\left(x - \frac{5}{x}\right)^2\left(1 + \frac{5}{x^2}\right)$$

16. Given that $\exp(2x^2 + 2y^2 - 16) = x + y$, find:

(a) $\dfrac{dy}{dx}$

(b) $\dfrac{dy}{dx}$ at $\left(\dfrac{1}{2}, \dfrac{1}{2}\right)$

Solution

$$\exp(2x^2 + 2y^2 - 16) = x + y$$

This can also be written as

$$e^{2x^2 + 2y^2 - 16} = x + y \qquad \text{(Note that } \exp x = e^x)$$

We now differentiate implicitly as follows:

$$\frac{d(2x^2 + 2y^2 - 16)}{dx} \times (e^{2x^2 + 2y^2 - 16}) = \frac{d(x)}{dx} + \frac{d(y)}{dx}$$

$$\left(4x + 4y\frac{dy}{dx}\right)(e^{2x^2 + 2y^2 - 16}) = 1 + \frac{dy}{dx}$$

Expanding the bracket gives:

$$4x(e^{2x^2 + 2y^2 - 16}) + 4y\frac{dy}{dx}(e^{2x^2 + 2y^2 - 16}) = 1 + \frac{dy}{dx}$$

Collecting terms in $\dfrac{dy}{dx}$ on the left hand side gives:

$$4y\frac{dy}{dx}(e^{2x^2 + 2y^2 - 16}) - \frac{dy}{dx} = 1 - 4x(e^{2x^2 + 2y^2 - 16})$$

Factorizing the left hand side gives:

$$\frac{dy}{dx}[4y(e^{2x^2 + 2y^2 - 16}) - 1] = 1 - 4x(e^{2x^2 + 2y^2 - 16})$$

Hence, $\quad \dfrac{dy}{dx} = \dfrac{1 - 4x(e^{2x^2 + 2y^2 - 16})}{4y(e^{2x^2 + 2y^2 - 16}) - 1}$

Or, $\quad \dfrac{dy}{dx} = \dfrac{-[4x(e^{2x^2 + 2y^2 - 16}) - 1]}{4y(e^{2x^2 + 2y^2 - 16}) - 1}$

(b) In order to find $\dfrac{dy}{dx}$ at $\left(\dfrac{1}{2} \ \dfrac{1}{2}\right)$, we simply substitute $x = \dfrac{1}{2}$ and $y = \dfrac{1}{2}$ into the expression for $\dfrac{dy}{dx}$ as follows:

$$\frac{dy}{dx} = \frac{-[4x(e^{2x^2 + 2y^2 - 16}) - 1]}{4y(e^{2x^2 + 2y^2 - 16}) - 1}$$

Since $x = \dfrac{1}{2}$ and $y = \dfrac{1}{2}$, this simplifies to give:

$$\frac{dy}{dx} \text{ at } \left(\frac{1}{2} \ \frac{1}{2}\right) = \frac{-[4\left(\frac{1}{2}\right)(e^{2x^2 + 2y^2 - 16}) - 1]}{4\left(\frac{1}{2}\right)(e^{2x^2 + 2y^2 - 16}) - 1}$$

$$= \frac{-[2(e^{2x^2 + 2y^2 - 16}) - 1]}{2(e^{2x^2 + 2y^2 - 16}) - 1}$$

The numerator cancels out the denominator to give:

$$\frac{dy}{dx} = \frac{-1}{1}$$

$$\frac{dy}{dx} = -1$$

17. If $y = x^3 - 2x^2 + 5$, show that: $x\dfrac{dy}{dx} - 3y - 2x^2 + 15 = 0$

Solution

$$y = x^3 - 2x^2 + 5$$

$$\frac{dy}{dx} = 3x^2 - 4x$$

Let us now simplify $x\dfrac{dy}{dx} - 3y - 2x^2 + 15$ as follows:

$$x\frac{dy}{dx} - 3y - 2x^2 + 15$$
$$= x(3x^2 - 4x) - 3y - 2x^2 + 15$$
$$= x(3x^2 - 4x) - 3(x^3 - 2x^2 + 5) - 2x^2 + 15 \quad \text{(Note that } x^3 - 2x^2 + 5 \text{ has been substituted for y)}$$
$$= 3x^3 - 4x^2 - 3x^3 + 6x^2 - 15 - 2x^2 + 15$$
$$= 0$$

Therefore, $x\dfrac{dy}{dx} - 3y - 2x^2 + 15 = 0$ as proven above.

18. Determine $\dfrac{d^2}{dx^2}\left(x\sin\dfrac{1}{x}\right)$

Solution

This means the second derivative of $x\sin\dfrac{1}{x}$

Let $y = x\sin\dfrac{1}{x}$

Or, $y = x\sin x^{-1}$

We now apply product rule to obtain $\dfrac{dy}{dx}$ as follows:

$$\frac{dy}{dx} = x\left[\frac{d(x^{-1})}{dx}\cos x^{-1}\right] + \sin x^{-1}\left[\frac{d(x)}{dx}\right]$$

$$= x(-x^{-2}\cos x^{-1}) + \sin x^{-1}(1)$$

$$= x\left(\frac{-1}{x^2}\cos x^{-1}\right) + \sin x^{-1}$$

$$= \frac{-x}{x^2}\cos x^{-1} + \sin x^{-1}$$

$$= \frac{-\cos x^{-1}}{x} + \sin x^{-1}$$

$$\frac{dy}{dx} = -\frac{1}{x}\cos\frac{1}{x} + \sin\frac{1}{x}$$

Or, $\dfrac{dy}{dx} = -x^{-1}\cos x^{-1} + \sin x^{-1}$

We now obtain $\dfrac{d^2y}{dx^2}$ as follows:

$$\frac{d^2y}{dx^2} = -x^{-1}\left[\frac{d(\cos x^{-1})}{dx}\right] + \cos x^{-1}\left[\frac{d(-x^{-1})}{dx}\right] + \frac{d(\sin x^{-1})}{dx}$$

$$= -x^{-1}\left[\frac{d(x^{-1})}{dx}(-\sin x^{-1})\right] + \cos x^{-1}(x^{-2}) + \left[\frac{d(x^{-1})}{dx}\cos x^{-1}\right]$$

$$= -x^{-1}[-x^{-2}(-\sin x^{-1})] + \cos x^{-1}(x^{-2}) - x^{-2}(\cos x^{-1})$$

$$= -x^{-1}(x^{-2}\sin x^{-1}) + x^{-2}\cos x^{-1} - x^{-2}\cos x^{-1}$$

$$= -x^{-1}(x^{-2}\sin x^{-1}) \quad \text{(Note that } x^{-2}\cos x^{-1} \text{ cancels out)}$$

$$= -x^{-3}\sin x^{-1}$$

$$\frac{d^2y}{dx^2} = -\frac{1}{x^3}\sin\frac{1}{x}$$

19. Given that $y = \dfrac{e^x + e^{-x}}{e^x - e^{-x}}$

(a) find $\dfrac{d^2y}{dx^2}$

(b) show that $\dfrac{d^2y}{dx^2} + 2y\dfrac{dy}{dx} = 0$

Solution

(a) $\quad y = \dfrac{e^x + e^{-x}}{e^x - e^{-x}}$

By using quotient rule we obtain $\dfrac{dy}{dx}$ as follows:

$$\frac{dy}{dx} = \frac{e^x - e^{-x}\left[\frac{d(e^x + e^{-x})}{dx}\right] - \left(e^x + e^{-x}\left[\frac{d(e^x - e^{-x})}{dx}\right]\right)}{(e^x - e^{-x})^2}$$

$$= \frac{(e^x - e^{-x})(e^x - e^{-x}) - (e^x + e^{-x})(e^x + e^{-x})}{(e^x - e^{-x})^2}$$

$$= \frac{(e^x - e^{-x})^2 - (e^x + e^{-x})^2}{(e^x - e^{-x})^2}$$

Separating into fractions gives:

$$= \frac{(e^x - e^{-x})^2}{(e^x - e^{-x})^2} - \frac{(e^x + e^{-x})^2}{(e^x - e^{-x})^2}$$

$$\frac{dy}{dx} = 1 - \frac{(e^x + e^{-x})^2}{(e^x - e^{-x})^2}$$

We now apply quotient and chain rules to obtain $\frac{d^2y}{dx^2}$ as follows:

$$\frac{d^2y}{dx^2} = 0 - \frac{(e^x - e^{-x})^2[2(e^x + e^{-x})(e^x - e^{-x})] - (e^x + e^{-x})^2[2(e^x - e^{-x})(e^x + e^{-x})]}{[(e^x - e^{-x})^2]^2}$$

$$= -\left[\frac{2(e^x - e^{-x})^3(e^x + e^{-x}) - 2(e^x + e^{-x})^3(e^x - e^{-x})}{(e^x - e^{-x})^4}\right]$$

$$= \frac{-2(e^x - e^{-x})^3(e^x + e^{-x}) + 2(e^x + e^{-x})^3(e^x - e^{-x})}{(e^x - e^{-x})^4}$$

$$= \frac{2(e^x + e^{-x})^3(e^x - e^{-x}) - 2(e^x - e^{-x})^3(e^x + e^{-x})}{(e^x - e^{-x})^4}$$

(After rearranging the numerator)

Separating into fractions gives:

$$= \frac{2(e^x + e^{-x})^3(e^x - e^{-x})}{(e^x - e^{-x})^4} - \frac{2(e^x - e^{-x})^3(e^x + e^{-x})}{(e^x - e^{-x})^4}$$

$$\frac{d^2y}{dx^2} = \frac{2(e^x + e^{-x})^3}{(e^x - e^{-x})^3} - \frac{2(e^x + e^{-x})}{e^x - e^{-x}}$$

(b) Let us simplify $\frac{d^2y}{dx^2} + 2y\frac{dy}{dx}$ as follows:

$$\frac{d^2y}{dx^2} + 2y\frac{dy}{dx}$$

$$= \frac{2(e^x + e^{-x})^3}{(e^x - e^{-x})^3} - \frac{2(e^x + e^{-x})}{e^x - e^{-x}} + 2\left(\frac{e^x + e^{-x}}{e^x - e^{-x}}\right)\left[1 - \frac{(e^x + e^{-x})^2}{(e^x - e^{-x})^2}\right]$$

Expanding bracket gives:

$$= \frac{2(e^x + e^{-x})^3}{(e^x - e^{-x})^3} - \frac{2(e^x + e^{-x})}{e^x - e^{-x}} + 2\left(\frac{e^x + e^{-x}}{e^x - e^{-x}}\right) - \frac{2(e^x + e^{-x})^3}{(e^x - e^{-x})^3}$$

$$= 0 \quad \text{(Since equal terms with opposite signs cancel out each other)}$$

Therefore, $\frac{d^2y}{dx^2} + 2y\frac{dy}{dx}$ gives zero as proven above.

Or, $\frac{d^2y}{dx^2} + 2y\frac{dy}{dx} = 0$

20. Find the derivative of ln(tan2x)

Solution

$y = \ln(\tan 2x)$

$$\frac{dy}{dx} = \frac{\frac{d(\tan 2x)}{dx}}{\tan 2x}$$

$$= \frac{2\sec^2 2x}{\tan 2x}$$

Or, $\dfrac{dy}{dx} = \dfrac{2\left(\frac{1}{\cos 2x}\right)\left(\frac{1}{\cos 2x}\right)}{\left(\frac{\sin 2x}{\cos 2x}\right)}$ (Note that $\sec 2x = \dfrac{1}{\cos 2x}$ and $\tan 2x = \dfrac{\sin 2x}{\cos 2x}$)

$$= \left(\frac{2}{\cos 2x}\right)\left(\frac{1}{\cos 2x}\right) \; \times \; \frac{\cos 2x}{\sin 2x}$$

$$\frac{dy}{dx} = \frac{2}{\sin 2x \cos 2x} \qquad \text{(Since } \cos 2x \text{ cancels } \cos 2x)$$

21. Given that $y = x^3 + 3x^2$, determine $2\dfrac{dy}{dx} - x\dfrac{d^2y}{dx^2}$

Solution

$$y = x^3 + 3x^2$$

$$\frac{dy}{dx} = 3x^2 + 6x$$

$$\frac{d^2y}{dx^2} = 6x + 6$$

Hence, $2\dfrac{dy}{dx} - x\dfrac{d^2y}{dx^2}$ is simplified as follows:

$$2(3x^2 + 6x) - x(6x + 6)$$

$$= 6x^2 + 12x - 6x^2 - 6x$$

$$= 6x$$

Therefore, $2\dfrac{dy}{dx} - x\dfrac{d^2y}{dx^2} = 6x$

22. Find $\dfrac{dy}{dx}$ if $y = 3(3x + \sqrt{x})^2$

Solution

$$y = 3(3x + \sqrt{x})^2$$

Applying chain rule gives:

$$\frac{dy}{dx} = 3 \; \times \; 2\,(3x + x^{\frac{1}{2}})^{2-1} \; \times \; \frac{d(3x + x^{\frac{1}{2}})}{dx} \qquad \text{(Note that } \sqrt{x} = x^{\frac{1}{2}})$$

$$= 6(3x + x^{\frac{1}{2}}) \; \times \; (3 + \frac{1}{2}x^{-\frac{1}{2}})$$

$$= 6(3x + x^{\frac{1}{2}})\left(3 + \frac{1}{2x^{\frac{1}{2}}}\right)$$

$$= 6(3x + \sqrt{x})\left(3 + \frac{1}{2\sqrt{x}}\right)$$

Expanding the bracket gives:

$$= 6\left(9x + \frac{3x}{2\sqrt{x}} + 3\sqrt{x} + \frac{1}{2}\right)$$

$$= 6\left(9x + \frac{3}{2}\sqrt{x} + 3\sqrt{x} + \frac{1}{2}\right) \qquad \left(\text{Note that } \frac{3x}{2\sqrt{x}} = \frac{3}{2}x^{1-\frac{1}{2}} = \frac{3}{2}x^{\frac{1}{2}} = 3\sqrt{x}\right)$$

$$= 6\left(9x + \frac{9}{2}\sqrt{x} + \frac{1}{2}\right)$$

$$\frac{dy}{dx} = 54x + 27\sqrt{x} + 3$$

23. If $y = \dfrac{5x^2 + 7}{x^4}$,

(a) find $\dfrac{d^2y}{dx^2}$

(b) show that $x^2\dfrac{d^2y}{dx^2} + 7x\dfrac{dy}{dx} + 8y = 0$

Solution

(a) $y = \dfrac{5x^2 + 7}{x^4}$

$$= \frac{5x^2}{x^4} + \frac{7}{x^4}$$

$$= \frac{5}{x^2} + \frac{7}{x^4}$$

$$y = 5x^{-2} + 7x^{-4}$$

$$\frac{dy}{dx} = -10x^{-3} - 28x^{-5}$$

Similarly,

$$\frac{d^2y}{dx^2} = 30x^{-4} + 140x^{-6}$$

(b) Let us now simplify $x^2\dfrac{d^2y}{dx^2} + 7x\dfrac{dy}{dx} + 8y$ by substituting appropriately as follows:

$$x^2(30x^{-4} + 140x^{-6}) + 7x(-10x^{-3} - 28x^{-5}) + 8(5x^{-2} + 7x^{-4})$$

$$= 30x^{-2} + 140x^{-4} - 70x^{-2} - 196x^{-4} + 40x^{-2} + 56x^{-4}$$

$$= 30x^{-2} + 40x^{-2} - 70x^{-2} + 140x^{-4} + 56x^{-4} - 196x^{-4}$$

$$= 0$$

Therefore $x^2\dfrac{d^2y}{dx^2} + 7x\dfrac{dy}{dx} + 8y$ gives zero as obtained above.

Or, $x^2\dfrac{d^2y}{dx^2} + 7x\dfrac{dy}{dx} + 8y = 0$

24. If $y = (2x + 5)^4 + \dfrac{x - 1}{2x - 1}$ find $\dfrac{dy}{dx}$.

Solution

$$(2x + 5)^4 + \frac{x - 1}{2x - 1}$$

We now use chain rule and quotient rule as follows:

$$\frac{dy}{dx} = 4(2x + 5)^{4-1} \times \frac{d(2x+5)}{dx} + \frac{(2x - 1)\frac{d(x-1)}{dx} - \left[(x - 1)\frac{d(2x-1)}{dx}\right]}{(2x - 1)^2}$$

$$= 4(2x + 5)^3(2) + \frac{(2x - 1)(1) - [(x - 1)(2)]}{(2x - 1)^2}$$

$$= 8(2x + 5)^3 + \frac{(2x - 1) - 2(x - 1)}{(2x - 1)^2}$$

$$= 8(2x + 5)^3 + \frac{2x - 1 - 2x + 2}{(2x - 1)^2}$$

$$\frac{dy}{dx} = 8(2x + 5)^3 + \frac{1}{(2x - 1)^2}$$

Exercise 17

1. If $y = x^2(3x^4 - 5)^3$ find $\frac{dy}{dx}$.

2. Given that $f(x) = 2x^5 - x^4 + 2x^3 + x^2 - 3x + 4$ find $f'(-2)$

3. A function $f(x)$ is given by $f(x) = \frac{\sqrt{(3x^2 - 1)^3}}{x^2}$. Find:

(a) the derivative of $f(x)$

(b) the gradient of $f(x)$ at the point $(1, -2)$

4. If $3xy^3 - y^2 - 4x^3 = 5y$, find:

(a) the derivative of the expression

(b) the gradient at $(-1, 1)$

5. Find the derivative of $(2x^2 + y^2)^2 = 0$

6. If $y = (x^2 + 5)^3(x^3 - 1)$, find $\frac{dy}{dx}$.

7. Find the derivative of $e^{\sin x + \tan x}$

8. Find the derivative of $\frac{x^2}{\sin^2 x}$

9. Differentiate with respect to x: $\ln(\sin^2 x + \cos 3x)$

10. If $y = a^{\cos 5x}$ find $\frac{dy}{dx}$.

11. Given that $y = x^2 e^{-3x}$ evaluate $\frac{d^2y}{dx^2} + \frac{dy}{dx} - y$

12. Differentiate with respect to x: $\sin\left(\frac{1 - 2x^3}{x^2}\right)$

13. If $y = \frac{2x - 1}{x^2}$, find $x^4\frac{d^2y}{dx^2} - 3(2x - 1)\frac{dy}{dx}$

14. Given that $y = 5e^{-2x} + 3e^x$, evaluate $\dfrac{d^2y}{dx^2} + \dfrac{dy}{dx} - 2y$

15. Find the derivative of $\left(\dfrac{1}{x^2} - \dfrac{2}{x}\right)^5$

16. Given that $e^{x^3 - y^3} = xy$, find:

(a) $\dfrac{dy}{dx}$

(b) $\dfrac{dy}{dx}$ at $(1, -1)$

17. If $y = \sin(\sin x)$, evaluate $\dfrac{d^2y}{dx^2} + \tan x\,\dfrac{dy}{dx} + y\cos^2 x$

18. Determine $\dfrac{d^2}{dx^2}\left(x^2\cos\dfrac{1}{x^2}\right)$

19. Given that $y = \dfrac{1 + e^{-x}}{1 - e^{-x}}$

(a) find $\dfrac{d^2y}{dx^2}$

(b) evaluate $\dfrac{d^2y}{dx^2} - \dfrac{dy}{dx} + y$

20. Find the derivative of $\ln(\sec^2 x)$

21. Given that $y = x + \tan x$, determine $\cos^2 x\,\dfrac{d^2y}{dx^2} - 2y + 2x$

22. Find $\dfrac{dy}{dx}$ if $y = \left(3x + \dfrac{\sqrt{5x}}{2}\right)^3$

23. If $y = \dfrac{x^3 + 2x^2 - 5x - 3}{x^2}$, find $\dfrac{d^2y}{dx^2}$

24. If $y = (x^3 + 1)^3 + \dfrac{5x - 2}{x^2 + 1}$ find $\dfrac{dy}{dx}$.

25. Given that $y = 2\cos 5x + 7\sin 5x$, determine $\dfrac{d^2y}{dx^2} + 25y$

ANSWERS TO EXERCISES

Exercise 1

1. 9   2. $-\dfrac{8}{5}$ 3. 9   4. 14   5. -14 6. $\dfrac{2}{5}$ 7. $\dfrac{1}{3}$ 8. -1 9. -15

10. 10   11. $\dfrac{1}{4}$ 12. 27   13. 12   14. $\dfrac{1}{10}$ 15. $\dfrac{3}{7}$ 16. Continuous

17. Continuous   18. Discontinuous   19. Not continuous (Discontinuous

20. Not continuous   21. Continuous   22. Not continuous   23. Not continuous

24(a) 8   (b) 5   26. $\dfrac{7}{2}$ 27. $\dfrac{1}{3}$ 28. 1   29. $-\dfrac{1}{2}$ 30. $2\dfrac{1}{4}$

Exercise 2

1. 2   2. $2x$ 3. $-3x^{-4}$ or $-\dfrac{3}{x^4}$ 4(a) $10x + 5h$ (b) $10x$

5(a) $27x^2 + 27xh + 9h^2$ (b) $27x^2$ 6(a) $\dfrac{2x^3 + 3x^2\Delta x + x(\Delta x)^2 + 2}{x(x + \Delta x)}$ (b) $2x + \dfrac{2}{x^2}$

7. $6x - 10$ 8. $1 - \dfrac{3}{x^2}$ 9. $5 - 6x$ 10. $2 + \dfrac{1}{5} = 2\dfrac{1}{5}$

Exercise 3

1(a) $40x^4$ (b) $2x^4$ (c) $\dfrac{1}{3x^{\frac{2}{3}}}$ or $\dfrac{1}{3\sqrt[3]{x^2}}$ (d) $\dfrac{1}{x^{\frac{6}{7}}}$ or $\dfrac{1}{\sqrt[7]{x^6}}$ (e) $-\dfrac{5}{8x^{\frac{13}{8}}}$ or $-\dfrac{5}{8\sqrt[8]{x^{13}}}$

(f) $-\dfrac{5}{x^{\frac{7}{2}}}$ or $-\dfrac{5}{\sqrt{x^7}}$ 2. (a) $10x^4 - 12x^3 - 12x^2 + 10x - 6$ (b) $7x^6 + 8x^3 + \dfrac{3}{x^2}$

(c) $18x^5 - 4x^3 - 5 - \dfrac{2}{x^2} + \dfrac{3}{x^4}$ (d) $\dfrac{5}{4\sqrt[4]{x^3}} - \dfrac{5}{3\sqrt[3]{2x^4}}$ 3. $8(2x - 5)^3$ 4. $\dfrac{-6}{(x^3 - 7)^3}$

5. $\dfrac{6x^2 + 7}{2(2x^3 + 7x)^{\frac{1}{2}}}$ 6. $5(21x^2 - 2x)(7x^3 - x^2 + 3)^4$ 7. $\left(9 + \dfrac{2}{x^2}\right)\left(3x - \dfrac{2}{3x}\right)^2$

8. $1 + \dfrac{9(6x - 1)}{(3x^2 - x - 10)^2}$ 9. $\dfrac{-4x^3}{\sqrt{1 - 2x^4}}$ 10. $\dfrac{-5x^2}{\sqrt[3]{(5x^3 - 1)^4}}$

Exercise 4

1. $12x - 1$ 2. $12x^3 + 50x$ 3. $\dfrac{15x + 30}{2\sqrt{3 + x}}$ 4. $(7x^2 + 30 - 7)(x^2 - 7)^2$

5. $48x^3 + 24x^2 - 6x - 20$ 6. $\dfrac{\sqrt{2}\,[(3x^2 - 1)^3 + 36x^2(9x^4 - 6x^2 + 1)]}{2\sqrt{x}}$

7. $\dfrac{15 - 7x}{4(x + 3)^{\frac{1}{4}}}$ or $\dfrac{15 - 7x}{4\sqrt[4]{x + 3}}$ 8. $12x^3 + 9x^2 - 46x - 5$ 9. $15x^4 - 12x^3 - 3x^2 + 6x - 2$

10. $\dfrac{12x + 1}{2}$ 11. $\dfrac{9x^{\frac{7}{2}}}{2}$ or $\dfrac{9\sqrt{x^7}}{2}$ 12. $\dfrac{4x^3(7x - 33)}{3\sqrt[3]{2x - 11}}$

13. $-30x^5 - 175x^4 + 20x^3 + 102x^2 - 14x + 1$ 14. $75x^4 + 28x^3 + 3x^2 + 28x - 7$

15. $-\dfrac{2}{x^2} + \dfrac{12}{x^5} - \dfrac{25}{x^6}$

Exercise 5

1. $\dfrac{x^2 - 2x + 4}{(x-1)^2}$ 2. $\dfrac{8x^2 + 24x - 3}{(2x+3)^2}$ 3. $\dfrac{42x}{(3x^2+1)^2}$ 4. $\dfrac{1}{(1-x)^{\frac{3}{2}}\sqrt{x+1}}$

5. $\dfrac{4(x^3-2)(x^3+1)}{x^3}$ 6. $\dfrac{-6(x^2+1)}{x^4\sqrt{3x^2+2}}$ 7. $\dfrac{-8x^2 + 12x + 24}{3(2x+1)^3(x^2-x-4)^{\frac{2}{3}}}$ 8. $\dfrac{10x^3 - 2x^2 - x + 4}{2(2-x)^{\frac{3}{2}}}$

9. $\dfrac{-6x}{(1-3x^2)^2}$ 10. $\dfrac{4}{(x-2)^2}$ or $\dfrac{4}{(2-x)^2}$

Exercise 6

1. $\dfrac{3t}{2}$ 2. $\dfrac{2(4-t^3)^2}{3t}$ 3. $\dfrac{2r}{3(l+2r)}$ 4. $\dfrac{2t-1}{10t-1}$ 5. $\dfrac{-2m(v-u)}{(u+v)t^2}$ 6. $\dfrac{5(t^4+1)^2}{3(t^2-1)^2}$

7. $\dfrac{1-12t^2}{2t}$ 8. $\dfrac{15t^2}{2}$ 9. $\dfrac{8}{r}$ 10. $\dfrac{2s^3}{3}$

Exercise 7

1. $\dfrac{-15x^2}{3-2y}$ or $\dfrac{15x^2}{2y-3}$ 2. $\dfrac{-4x}{9y^2}$ 3. $\dfrac{3y^2 + 12x^2 - y}{x - 6xy}$ 4. $\dfrac{3x^2 - y^2 - 4x}{2xy}$ 5. $\dfrac{x^2}{y}$

6. $\dfrac{4xy}{2x^2+5}$ 7. $\dfrac{-2xy}{x^2+6y^2-1}$ 8. $\dfrac{4y}{10y-4x-1}$ 9. $\dfrac{2xy^2-1}{2y(x^2-1)}$ 10. $\dfrac{-5x^4y^2}{3}$

Exercise 8

1. $2\sec^2 2x$ 2. $-\dfrac{1}{5}\sin\dfrac{1}{5}x$ 3. $-50\sin 5x$ 4. $3\sin^2 x\cos x$ 5. $2\sec^2 x\tan x$

6. $60x^4\sin^3 3x^5\cos 3x^5$ 7. $-12x\cot 6x^2\csc 6x^2$ 8. $10x^4\sec 2x^5\tan 2x^5$ 9. $6x\sec^2 3x^2$

10. $-x(3x\sin 3x - 2\cos 3x)$ 11. $\dfrac{6x\cos 2x - 9\sin 2x}{x^4}$ 12. $48x^3\sec x^4\tan x^4$

13. $\dfrac{-5\tan x\cos 5x - \sec^2 x(2 - \sin 5x)}{\tan^2 x}$ 14. $\dfrac{\sin^2 x(3x\cos x - \sin x)}{2x^2}$

15. $\dfrac{-(2x+6)\csc^2 2x - \cot 2x)}{(x+3)^2}$ 16. $\dfrac{-\sin^3\sqrt{3}}{5x^2}$ 17. $\dfrac{2[x - (x^2-3)\tan 2x]}{\sec 2x}$

18. $6x\cos 3x^2 - 18x^3\sin 3x^2$ 19. $-\cos x(2\cot x\sin x + \cos x\csc^2 x)$

20. $\dfrac{2(\sin^2 x + \sin^2 x)}{(\sin x + \cos x)^2}$ or $\dfrac{2}{(\sin x + \cos x)^2}$ 21. $\dfrac{4\sec 4x\sin(4x-2) + \tan 4x\cos(4x-2)}{\cos^2(4x-2)}$

22. $-3\sin 3x - x^2\sec x\tan x - 2x\sec x$ 23. $27x^2\cos x^3\sin^8 x^3$ 24. $\dfrac{3\cos 6\sqrt{x}}{\sqrt{x}}$

25. $3\cos x^3 - \dfrac{2\sin x^3}{x^3}$ 26. $-30x^4\cos^2 2x^5\sin 2x^2$ 27. $-10\sin 2x\sin 10x - 2\cos 2x\cos 10x$

28. $6x^2\cos x^4 - \dfrac{3\sin x^4}{2x^2}$ 29. $\dfrac{(10x-5)\sec^2 5x - 2\tan 5x}{(2x-1)^2}$ 30. $\dfrac{\sec^2 x\tan x}{x} - \dfrac{\tan^2 x}{2x^2}$

Exercise 9

1. $\dfrac{1}{3\sqrt[3]{7y^2}}$ 2. $\dfrac{3y^2}{2\sqrt{y^3-1}}$ 3. $\dfrac{1}{5\sqrt[5]{2(y+3)^4}}$ 4. $\dfrac{1}{\sqrt[3]{2(3y+27)^2}}$ 5. $\dfrac{-1}{(y-2)^2}$

6. $\dfrac{-3}{2y^2\sqrt{\dfrac{3}{y}+5}}$ 7. $2y^3$ 8. $5y^4$ 9. $\dfrac{-5}{(y-4)^2}$ 10. $\dfrac{-1}{3y^2\sqrt[3]{(\frac{1}{y}+8)^2}}$

Exercise 10

1. $\dfrac{2}{\sqrt{1-4x^2}}$ 2. $\dfrac{-1}{\sqrt{1-x^2}}$ 3. $\dfrac{-6x}{9x^4+1}$ 4. $\dfrac{-4x^3}{x^8+1}$ 5. $3\sec^{-1}x+\dfrac{3}{\sqrt{x^2-1}}$

6. $2x+\dfrac{3}{x^2+1}$ 7. $\dfrac{1}{(x+5)^2+1}$ or $\dfrac{1}{x^2+10x+26}$ 8. $\dfrac{1}{x^2\sqrt{1-\dfrac{1}{x^2}}}$ 9. $\dfrac{-1}{5\sqrt{1-y^2}}$

10. $\dfrac{1}{2y\sqrt{y-1}}$ 11. $5\tan^{-1}3x+\dfrac{15x}{9x^2+1}$ 12. $2x+\dfrac{20x^4}{\sqrt{1-x^{10}}}$ 13. $\dfrac{-3}{x\sqrt{x^6-1}}$

14. $\dfrac{1}{2(y^2+1)}$ 15. $\dfrac{1}{15y^{\frac{2}{3}}\sqrt{1-y^{\frac{2}{3}}}}$

Exercise 11

1. $3\cosh3x-2\sinh x$ 2. $-5x\operatorname{sech}x(x\tanh x-2)$ 3. $\dfrac{2(x\cosh 2x-\sinh 2x)}{3x^3}$

4. $6\cosh3x\sinh3x$ 5. $60x^4\cosh^24x^5\sinh4x^5$ 6. $-10x^4\operatorname{cosech}2x^5$

7. $-12x\operatorname{sech}^32x^2\tanh2x^2$ 8. $x(5x\sinh5x+2\cosh5x)$

9. $\dfrac{3\operatorname{cosech}^23x\tanh 5x+5\coth 3x\operatorname{sech}^25x}{\coth^23x}$ 10. $\dfrac{2\cosh^2x(3x\sinh x-\cosh x)}{3x^2}$

Exercise 12

1. $\dfrac{1}{x}\log_a e$ 2. $\dfrac{3x^2}{x^3+5}\log_a e$ 3. $\dfrac{36x^2}{2x^3-5}\log_a e$ 4. $\dfrac{2}{3x}\log_a e$ 5. $\dfrac{4x}{(x^2+1)(1-x^2)}\log_a e$

or $\dfrac{-4x}{(x^2+1)(x^2-1)}\log_a e$ or $\dfrac{-4x}{(x^4-1)}\log_a e$ 6. $\dfrac{15x^2}{5x^3-1}\log_5 e$ 7. $\dfrac{-2}{x}\log_2 e$ 8. $\dfrac{2x}{x^2+3}$

9. $\dfrac{3\ln^2x}{x}$ 10. $\dfrac{5x^4}{2x^5-1}$ 11. $2x^3(4\ln x+1)$ 12. $\dfrac{-28}{3-7x}$ or $\dfrac{28}{7x-3}$

13. $6x\ln(4x^3+1)+\dfrac{36x^4}{4x^3+1}$ 14. $\dfrac{2-4\ln x}{x^3}$ 15. $\dfrac{-30x}{1-5x^2}$ or $\dfrac{30x}{5x^2-1}$

Exercise 13

1. $10a^{2x}\log_e a$ 2. $a^{5x^2-x}\ln a(10x-1)$ 3. $a^{3x}x^3(3x\ln a+4)$

4. $-2e^{-2x}-3e^{-x}$ or $-e^{-2x}(2+3e^x)$ 5. $\dfrac{\sqrt{3}\,e^{\sqrt{3x}}}{\sqrt{x}}$ 6. $6x^2e^{x^2}(2x^2+3)$

7. $\dfrac{5\ln a\,(a^{10x}-1)}{a^{5x}}$ 8. $\dfrac{6e^{4x}(2x\ln 2x^2+1)}{x}$ 9. $\dfrac{3x\sqrt{e^{5x}}(5x+4)}{2a}$ 10. $x^3(\log_{10}e+4\log_{10}7x)$

150

11. $3\ln6(6^{3x})$ 12. $2x - 3(e^{x^2 - 3x})$ 13. $\dfrac{-(5x + 3)e^{\frac{3}{x}}}{5x^7}$ 14. $6e^{-3x}$

15. $3(2x + 1)(x^2 + x)^2 e^{(x^2 + x)^3}$ 16. $2^{x^2} 2x \ln2$ 17. $2a^{2x}\ln a$ 18. $\dfrac{e^x(x\ln 10 x^3 + 3)}{x}$

19. $\dfrac{\sqrt{5}(4x + 1)e^{2x}}{2\sqrt{x}}$ 20. $2x^4(4\log_{10}e + 5\log_{10}5x^4)$

Exercise 14

1. $x^{2x}(2 + 2\ln x)$ 2. $\dfrac{3x^{\ln 2x}(\ln 2x + \ln x)}{x}$ 3. $\ln(1 - 4x^2) - \dfrac{8x^2}{1 - 4x^2}$

4. $(6x^x - 5)^{3x}\left[3\ln(6x^2 - 5) + \dfrac{36x^2}{6x^2 - 5}\right]$ 5. $\dfrac{(2x^3 + 1)(x - 2)^3}{3x^2(x^3 - 1)^2}\left(\dfrac{6x^2}{2x^3 + 1} + \dfrac{3}{x - 2} - \dfrac{2}{x} - \dfrac{6x^2}{x^3 - 1}\right)$

6. $\dfrac{(2x - 1)(x^2 - 2)}{(1 - x)(x - 3)^2}\left(\dfrac{2}{2x - 1} + \dfrac{2x}{x^2 - 2} + \dfrac{1}{1 - x} - \dfrac{2}{x - 3}\right)$

7. $15x^3 x^{3x^4}(4\ln x + 1)$ or $15x^{3x^4 + 3}(4\ln x + 1)$ 8. $3e^{3x}(e^{e^{3x}})$ or $3e^{e^{3x} + 3x}$

9. $2^{e^x}e^x\ln2$ 10. $\dfrac{x^{\ln(x^2 - 4x)}[(x - 4)\ln(x^2 - 4x) + (2x - 4)\ln x]}{x(x - 4)}$ 11. $\ln(2x^2 + 10) + \dfrac{4x^2}{2x^2 + 10}$

12. $(3x^2 - 8)^{2x}\left[2\ln(3x^3 - 8) + \dfrac{18x^3}{3x^3 - 8}\right]$ 13. $\dfrac{(x + 3)^2(x - 3)^2}{x^3 - 1}\left(\dfrac{2}{x + 3} + \dfrac{2}{x - 3} - \dfrac{3x^2}{x^3 - 1}\right)$

14. $15x^{(\ln x)^2}(\ln x)^2$ 15. $30x^{3x^2}x(2\ln x + 1)$ or $30x^{3x^2 + 1}(2\ln x + 1)$

Exercise 15

1. $\dfrac{3}{5x^2}$ 2. $\dfrac{5xe^{5x}}{2}$ 3. $\dfrac{-2x\sin x^2}{\cos x}$ 4. $\dfrac{x(6x - 5)}{x - 1}$ 5. $\dfrac{14x^2}{3}$ 6. $\dfrac{2a^x\ln a}{e^x}$

7. $\dfrac{-2\tan x \sec^2 x}{5\sin 5x}$ 8. $\dfrac{1}{(x - 1)(e^{x-1})}$ 9. $\dfrac{1}{xe^{5x}}$ 10. $\dfrac{e^x + e^{-x}}{(e^x - e^{-x})(1 + \ln x)}$

Exercise 16

1. $\dfrac{dy}{dx} = 2x(2x^2 - 3x - 7)$, $\dfrac{d^2y}{dx^2} = 2(6x^2 - 6x - 7)$, $\dfrac{d^3y}{dx^3} = 2(12x - 6)$ 2. $-\dfrac{3}{x^2}$

3. $20x^2 e^{5x^4}(20x^4 + 3)$ 4. $-50x^8\sin^2 x^5 + 40x^3\cos x^5\sin x^5 + 50x^8\cos x^5$ 5. $\dfrac{128}{(4x - 10)^2}$

6. $\dfrac{-(x^2 - 2)\sin x - 2x\cos x}{x^3}$ 7. $\dfrac{4\ln x - 6}{x^3}$ 8. $-2\csc^2 x(\csc^2 x + 2\cot^2 x)$

9. $2\cos^2 x - 3\sin^2 x - 5\cos 2x$ 10. 0

11. $-8x^2\sin x^2 + 4\cos x^2 + 2\sin^2 x - 2\cos^2 x - 4x\cos x^2 + 2\cos x\sin x$

12. $\dfrac{2[(x^2\sec^2 x + 1)\tan x - x\sec^2 x]}{3x^3}$ 13. $e^{-x}(4\sin 2x - 3\cos 2x)$ 14. 0

15. $\dfrac{-(9x^2 - 2)\sin 3x - 6x\cos 3x}{3x^3}$

151

Exercise 17

1. $2x(3x^4 - 5)^3 + 36x(3x^4 - 5)^3$ or $2x(3x^4 - 5)^2(21x^4 - 5)$ 2. 209

3(a) $\dfrac{\sqrt{3x^2 - 1}\,(3x^2 + 2)}{x^3}$ (b) $5\sqrt{2}$ 4(a) $\dfrac{12x^2 - 3y^3}{9xy^2 - 2y - 5}$ (b) $-\dfrac{9}{16}$ 5. $-\dfrac{2}{y}$

6. $3x(x^2 + 5)^2(3x^3 + 5x - 2)$ 7. $e^{\sin x + \tan x}(\sec^2 x + \cos x)$ 8. $\dfrac{2x(\sin x - x\cos x)}{\sin^3 x}$

9. $\dfrac{2\cos x \sin x - 3\sin 3x}{\sin^2 x + \cos 3x}$ 10. $-5a^{\cos 5x}\sin 5x \ln a$ 11. $5x^2\,e^{-3x} - 10xe^{-3x} + 2e^{-3x}$

12. $-(2x^3 + 2)\cos\left(\dfrac{1 - 2x^3}{x^2}\right)$ 13. $\dfrac{4x^4 - 6x^3 + 12x^2 - 18x + 6}{x^3}$ 14. 0

15. $5\left(\dfrac{2}{x^2} - \dfrac{2}{x^3}\right)\left(\dfrac{1}{x^2} - \dfrac{2}{x}\right)^4$ or $\dfrac{10(x-1)(1-2x)^4}{x^{11}}$ 16(a) $\dfrac{3x^2 e^{x^3 - y^3} - y}{3y^2 e^{x^3 - y^3} + x}$ (b) 1

17. 0   18. $\dfrac{2\sin\frac{1}{x^2}}{x^2} - \dfrac{4\cos\frac{1}{x^2}}{x^4} + 2\cos\dfrac{1}{x^2}$ 19(a) $\dfrac{2e^x(e^x + 1)}{(e^x - 1)^3}$

(b) $\dfrac{4(e^{2x} - e^{-x}) + (1 + e^{-x})(e^x - 1)^3}{(e^x - 1)^3(1 - e^{-x})}$ 20. $2\tan x$ 21. 0

22. $3\left(\dfrac{\sqrt{5}}{4\sqrt{x}} + 3\right)\left(3x + \dfrac{\sqrt{5x}}{2}\right)^2$ 23. $\dfrac{-10x - 18}{x^4}$ or $\dfrac{-2(5x + 9)}{x^4}$

24. $9x^2(x^3 + 1)^2 + \dfrac{5 + 4x - 10x^2}{(x^2 + 1)^2}$ 25. 0

Please if you found this book well simplified enough for easier understanding, kindly give it a five star rating on amazon so as to encourage people to buy this book, thereby helping them improve on their skills on differential calculus. Thank you.

If you have any enquiry, suggestion or information concerning this book, please contact the author through the email below.

KINGSLEY AUGUSTINE

kingzohb2@yahoo.com

Printed in Great Britain
by Amazon

37789158R00086